Potty Training

*The Easy and Effective Method
for Teaching Your Child*

Author: Pamela C. Walker

Table of Contents

Book Description: Potty Training

A big moment for parents and children alike, potty training is a process that *can* be made easy. By using this guide, you will learn how to prepare your child for the milestone of using the bathroom while creating lifelong habits to assist them. Getting rid of the fear and intimidation is the first step toward making sure that your child is comfortable enough to assert the independence necessary for learning how to use the bathroom and getting out of diapers for good. Starting from the very beginning, you will learn what signs to look for in order to determine if your child is ready to be potty trained. While keeping in mind that all children develop differently, you will be able to tell exactly when the time is right for your child. The techniques covered are meant to be fun and interesting to children, encouraging them to actually *want* to use the toilet and to apply their self-sufficient behavior. Without any fear tactics or punishment involved, you will be able to put your trust in your child as you teach them everything that they need to know about potty training. This guide is meant to help you along the way, answering questions and providing you with inspiration.

1

Introduction

A pivotal moment in any child's life, potty training is one of the first big milestones that will allow more independence. As your child approaches the point where they appear ready, it is your duty as a parent to assist with making an easy transition from diapers to the toilet. Given the helpful tips that are provided in this guide, both you and your child will have the most positive experience with potty training. Because all children are different in terms of their desire and ability to start using the toilet, you will need to make a plan that is flexible and nurturing. With the use of positive reinforcement and creative techniques, your child will have the confidence that they need in order to learn all of the necessary steps. This success comes from your child's willingness to participate and your open-minded approach.

Getting rid of the pressure that surrounds the topic, you will learn if your child is ready by assessing their individual traits. Potty training is not black and white; it is a process that can look different for each family. It is important to remember that patience is the foundation of any milestone. The energy that you provide your child with is the energy that they are going to mirror. This is why staying calm and patient is essential when you are potty training. There are going to be some setbacks along the way, but if you are able to prepare yourself and your child adequately, you will both be able to overcome them with ease. Once you begin the process, you are already one step closer to achieving your potty training goals.

If your child is walking, this is one of the first indications that they are ready to hold themselves up enough to sit on the toilet. A transitional toilet seat might be necessary at first. Children's potty training seats are smaller and easier to use in the beginning. Without having a fear of falling in, your child can experience what it feels like to use the bathroom without a diaper. A lot of parents like to participate in this step, but it is not mandatory for successful potty training. These children's toilets can be a great way for your child to build up the confidence to use standard toilets in the future. The decision to use one in your process will be determined by how ready you perceive your child to be.

The first time your child uses the bathroom without a diaper on, you should do your best to reinforce this behavior with proper praising and a rewards system. Potty training can be fun for both the child and the parent; it is a myth that this is a difficult task. Utilizing this guide, you are going to prepare a plan for your child to follow. As long as you are able to keep them on track, you should start noticing the results right away. It is a milestone that every child is going to experience, and this book encourages the easiest method possible to ensure that potty training will be accomplished. Without the stress of trying to get it done in a certain amount of time, you will both enjoy learning this next step together, and you will see that it can actually be fun!

Chapter 1
When to Potty Train

"You can learn many things from children. How much patience you have, for instance."

-Franklin P. Jones, American humorist

The biggest question that you will probably have in the beginning is if the time is right. How can you ensure that it is time to begin potty training? The answer is not going to be the same for all children. On average, children begin to show signs that they are ready between the ages of 18-24 months. Again, just because this is the average age does not necessarily mean that your child will begin showing these signs as well. Some children are not ready until they are up to 3-years-old, and that is okay. Know that these are the parameters for you to keep in mind. The main thing to keep in mind is that your child might not be able to retain the information if you start too early. If you notice that some of the signs are present early on, it could be a wise decision to wait a few more months until you notice all of them.

No matter what you decide, know that there is no rush. Potty training is a process that will never happen overnight, and it requires a sense of dedication. While you want to see your child succeed, you also know your child best. Introduce the concept by talking about it frequently. Be open with your child by allowing them to become familiar with the bathroom and what happens in it. Creating a sense of curiosity is a great way to jumpstart any of the signs that are already present. This step can begin as soon as your child is able to comprehend the concept, even if they are nowhere near ready to start potty training. It is a way to introduce the toilet so that you do not have to on day one of your training process.

How to Know if Your Child is Ready

As mentioned, there are certain signs children exhibit that indicate they are ready to start potty training. These are some of the most common that you should be paying attention to as your child gets older:

- Walking: It takes balance for your child to hold themselves up and walk. Without this balance, potty training becomes difficult because you will have to hold them up as they sit on the toilet. This method brings a sense of ease to the process, so this is an important aspect of being ready. By potty training, you are aiming to bring more independence into your child's life. Know that this is far more likely to happen when they can sit on a children's toilet or a standard toilet on their own.

- Getting Dressed: Being able to pull their pants up and down on their own is another great sign that indicates potty training is possible. This is something that your child needs to be able to master in order to use the bathroom independently. It helps to dress your child in bottoms that do not require any fastening. Anything that can be quickly and easily pulled on is preferred for both your child and you when you begin potty training.

- Staying Dry: When you start to notice that your child's diaper stays dry for up to 2 hours at a time, this is a great sign. It means that their bladder is developing in a way that they will be able to control the frequency with which they must use the bathroom. If you are still changing their diaper more than this, then it might be a good idea to give them some more time before starting the training.

- Communication: Talking is an essential aspect of potty training. Even if your child is still developing the skills necessary to formulate complete sentences, some form of communication is necessary for them to be able to tell you when they need to use the bathroom. Otherwise, you will simply be guessing for them. Being able to communicate these needs or even point to the bathroom is a way for your child to take control of the situation.

- Following Instructions: Between the ages of 1-3 years, your child should be able to follow your instructions. From knowing how to clean up their toys to eating properly, it is around this time when you are going to be teaching your child cues that they must follow. Potty training is the same way--you are going to be giving instructions. A responsive child is going to appear obedient and potentially curious. They might ask you why they need to use the bathroom or other questions that are related to the process.

- Interest: As mentioned, curiosity is a great thing. When your child becomes curious about the toilet and wants to walk into the bathroom, this shows you that there is an interest developing. Always encourage this behavior as much as you can. It is during this time that you will also introduce the idea of privacy. Teach your child that what happens in the bathroom is important yet private. Explain all of the items inside of the room and how to use them. This will answer a lot of questions that your child might have.

Keeping these indicators in mind, allow these to be the standards that you follow. If you notice one or more of these signs, then the time is probably right for you to begin potty training. It is a long process of trial and error, so don't be disappointed if you accidentally misread the timing. When you notice an even split between these signs, the best thing that you can probably do is wait a little bit longer. Make sure to check and see if your child has progressed with any of the other indications. This time in your child's life is going to fly by pretty quickly; when they don't appear ready, you mind find that they are suddenly exhibiting all of the signs within the next month.

Your keen attention to detail is important here. As the parent, trust in your ability to know what is best for your child. As long as you are listening to the signs, this pre-potty training time is going to be one that is enjoyable to explore. Never shame your child for not being ready, and never blame yourself either. Potty training can only happen when it naturally makes sense. It is one of the main things in parenting that you cannot force to happen sooner. The best thing that you can do as you wait until the time is right is to be as open as possible with your child. Allow them to ask questions about using the bathroom and teach them about the process whenever you can.

No one else can make this determination except for you, so you must have as much trust in yourself as you have in your child. Parenting involves a lot of decision-making where you must feel confident so that your child can feel confident. One of the easiest ways to become stressed out is by second-guessing your judgment. Your child is going to be expressing these signs, and as long as you know what you are looking for, you will be able to prepare both of you for the journey that is potty training.

Do You Have Everything You Need?

Once you determine that your child is ready to begin potty training, you must decide if you would like to use a potty chair or children's toilet. These are two transitional tools that make it easier and less intimidating for your child to use the bathroom. Although they are not meant to be used for a long time, just a little bit of work with them can help tremendously. There is no benefit between using one of these items and not using one; the choice is up to you and what you believe is best for your child. See if it seems like they are interested enough to sit on the regular toilet without being scared or worried about falling in. You will likely need to help them first to show them what it feels like.

These first few experiences will allow you to gauge whether you should use the above-mentioned training items or not. A potty chair is great because it is convenient, and it does not take up too much space in your bathroom. The attachment clips onto any standard toilet, allowing for a secure and smaller toilet for your child to use. It can be left on the toilet and easily unclipped for when the adults need to use the bathroom. They are also fairly inexpensive when it comes to potty training equipment. No matter if you have a boy or a girl, the easiest way to begin using the regular toilet is on a potty chair. Depending on the gender, the way that you teach your child to get onto the seat and to aim will vary, but the convenience will be the same.

Using a stool is another way to make your child's potty training experience more comfortable. Since your child likely won't be able to touch the ground when they are sitting on the regular toilet, placing a stool at their feet will allow them to feel safe and secure. It takes away the feeling that they might fall, and it can also help them to get onto the toilet comfortably. A stool is another convenient tool because it can be stowed away underneath the sink or in the cabinet. Whenever your child needs to use the bathroom, it can be easily pulled right back out.

A children's toilet is a separate toilet that normally sits on the floor beside the regular toilet in your bathroom. It contains a shallow pan that you must manually empty, which is something that you should keep in mind. These toilets usually come in bright colors featuring various cartoon characters to get your child more interested in potty training. They are compact and a lot less intimidating if the potty chair is just too advanced for right now. A lot of parents opt for both things, in the beginning, to see which one their child favors. Children learn fast when it comes to potty training, so don't worry about using one more than the other. They will both likely be used and then outgrown before you know it.

Consider getting a faucet extender. When your child is done using the bathroom, washing their hands can prove to be the next challenge that must be faced. Because most faucets are out of reach to children, a stool and a faucet extender are going to be very helpful. This is an essential item if you are keen on teaching your child about proper hygiene at an early age. Always promote the idea of washing their hands after each visit to the bathroom in order to avoid the spread of germs and bacteria. A child that learns these habits early on will remember them as they grow older.

Aside from the physical items that are necessary to potty train with, you will want to consider switching your child over to pull-ups. This diaper/underwear hybrid is going to make it easier when your child begins to wear underwear. They come on and off easily, allowing the child the independence of being able to dress themselves. Also, they are less absorbent than diapers, so you need to ensure that your child can stay dry for a few hours at a time. Again, using these is only a suggestion, but they are known to make the process of potty training easier for both yourself and your child.

The literature on potty training can be helpful, too. There are many great books on the topic that you can read to your child to encourage them to begin using the toilet. This builds up curiosity and makes the idea of potty training more fun. If you wish, you can also stock up on small rewards that can be given each time the bathroom is used instead of a diaper. The rewards can be little toys or treats that your child will begin to look forward to. If you don't want to provide a reward after each time that they use the bathroom, you can make it a weekly thing-- a toy reward for each week of great bathroom usage.

Tips for an Easy Transition

Getting started with potty training is like one big experiment. You are going to learn about your child's habits and bathroom schedule. Once you observe this enough, you should be able to create a daily routine that involves bathroom breaks. No matter what you have in store each day, try to schedule bathroom breaks around the same time and during the same intervals. This will keep your child regulated while giving them a fair chance at using the toilet. Remember, if this just doesn't happen at first, don't feel discouraged. There might not be enough interest behind the idea of using the bathroom, or it might be too intimidating. You will need to see how your child feels.

In order to learn the feeling of needing to go, your child will need some time to get the hang of this. It is a good idea to let them sit on the toilet for longer period until that feeling is apparent. Sit in there with them, providing them with games to play and books to read. This is probably going to be the most time-consuming part of your potty training method, but it will allow your child to know exactly what it feels like when they need to go. Be patient, even if the feeling doesn't come up. Think of it this way--you are still practicing important skills that are necessary for using the toilet. Each time your child sits down on a toilet rather than in a diaper is going to be an improvement and one step closer to independence.

Act quickly when you notice the signs that they need to go. Whether your child lets you know, or you simply understand the non-verbal cues to look out for, try to get to the bathroom as quickly as you can. The urgency behind using the bathroom is going to feel more intense to your child than it will feel to you. Be mindful of this as you try to get them to the bathroom as quickly as you can. The more experience that your child gets with holding it, the more that they will be able to do so. Only practice can make this possible. You cannot expect them to become potty-trained overnight, so make sure that you are being as calm and patient as you can.

After a few weeks of success with potty training, you can get rid of diapers altogether. This might feel like a big step, and that is because it is! Allow your child to have the confidence in knowing that they can use the bathroom instead of relying on diapers. Make sure that you introduce underwear in an exciting way and allow them to pick out some pairs that they like. The more that you can build up the desire to wear underwear, the more that your child will want to use the bathroom. Accidents will happen, and that is okay. You do not need to shame or punish your child for them, as they are natural. Try to remind them to pay attention to the signs of needing to go, clean the dirty underwear, and keep moving forward with your training.

Nighttime is one of the most challenging times when it comes to potty training. This is the longest that your child will go without using the bathroom. A lot of children like to use the bathroom when they first wake up in the morning, and it can be hard to remember that it must be held until they are on the toilet. Pull-ups can bridge this gap at first, providing some security until you find get your child inside the bathroom. They won't always be necessary, though. You must observe how well your child is doing and notice how often they wet the bed.

No matter when the toilet is being used, always place an emphasis on hygiene. Again, this lesson might look different depending on if you are potty training a boy or a girl. For boys, introducing standing while they pee can be a messy challenge. You need to teach them to aim properly, and always remind them to wash their hands when they are through. Girls must learn which direction to wipe in order to avoid infections. Teaching them at a young age is a way to ensure that they are going to practice these same habits as they grow up. Again, place emphasis on handwashing. Never feel embarrassed about talking to your child about these things. They are all-natural practices of human beings, and if you do not teach them, then they aren't going to learn properly. It is your job as the parent to bring clarity to the topic of potty training.

If you are going to be out of the house for some time, potty training can prove to be difficult. Always bring a backup pair of underwear or pull-ups with you in case of an accident. Allow your child the time to use the bathroom before you leave the house, explaining that there might not be an easily accessible bathroom for quite some time. If you do need to utilize a public restroom, you won't have your potty chair or children's toilet with you. In this case, you will probably have to assist your child by holding them as they use the bathroom. Just like at home, make sure that they wipe if necessary and clean their hands properly when they are finished.

Chapter 2
Dealing with Accidents

"Children are likely to live up to what you believe of them."

-Lady Bird Johnson, former First Lady of the United States

An inevitable part of potty training, knowing what to do when your child has an accident is going to keep the momentum going. Accidents are expected because it is uncommon that your child is going to grasp the concept of using the bathroom overnight. There are several different factors that you must overcome when you are potty training. Sometimes, even when you have a combination of all these things, accidents can still happen. Remember that this is a very new change for your child.

While you cannot do anything that will ensure that your child will not have any accidents, what you can do is prepare yourself to handle them. As a parent, you are going to act as a support system. You must be ready to clean up after your child while not making them feel guilty or ashamed. Accidents are natural, so treat them as such. Reassure your child that it is okay and help them get cleaned up as best as you can. If an accident happens in public, this can cause a lot of embarrassment. This is why you must be ready with proper supplies at all times. During potty training, you are going to need to bring a bag with you that is similar to a diaper bag. This will act as a safety net in case an accident does happen.

Accidents that happen at home can be turned into a learning experience. While you do want to help your child get cleaned up, you can also take the time to find out what they felt before the accident happened. Let them think about the feeling of needing to go so that they can recognize it again in the future. After explaining that this is a normal feeling, you can allow your child to dress themselves and get ready to try again. Sometimes it does take a few accidents in order for your child to really know what feeling they should be waiting for before using the bathroom.

What to Do

As soon as your child has an accident, the first step is to get them feeling comfortable and confident again. There is no need to delay this process because this will allow the self-doubt to begin. You do not want to ruin your child's desire to use the bathroom again in the future, so try to not make accidents seem scary or bad. As you are helping your child get cleaned up, explain how accidents are normal. Allow your child to see that your energy is calm and that you are not mad. Though it can be frustrating, especially when you think that potty training has already been accomplished, it really is a normal experience and a big part of the process.

The next step is to evaluate why the accident happened. You can ask your child about this, but too much interrogation could result in embarrassment. Ask gently about it and why he believes that it happened. Don't be surprised if they cannot give you an exact answer; it can be a confusing experience. Do your best to evaluate the situation on your own--think about the last time that your child used the bathroom. When the accident happened, were they doing something exciting? Did they just wake up from a nap? Keep track of the way that they all occur in order to notice a pattern. You might be able to prevent them from happening again in the future if you can find out what is triggering them.

A common misconception is that accidents mean your child is regressing--this isn't always the case. Once they have the concept of potty training down, it is very rare for them to throw all of these skills away. Children are observant and great learners. It might just take some time for them to feel comfortable utilizing these skills again. As much as you do not want to be too hard on your child for having an accident, you also don't want to be hard on yourself as a parent. This is not an indication that you have failed your child, so don't treat it as such. The best way to handle an accident is to keep a lighthearted approach to it. From the way that you clean up after one to the way that you talk to your child and provide words of encouragement to try again, this should all be done in a calm and soothing manner.

If you notice that accidents keep happening, consider trying to put your child in pull-ups for a short period of time. This small step acts as a safeguard until you see that your child is ready to start wearing underwear again and using the bathroom. Again, this is not an indication of regression. It simply means that you must modify your potty training in order to fit your child's needs. There is no telling what might trigger an accident, so it makes sense for you to provide your child with some safety and reassurance until they feel confident enough to try again. Don't feel that you have to go back to diapers; this is taking too many steps back. Utilizing pull-ups is going to be enough.

Make note of any environmental changes that have occurred during the time of the accidents. These changes can make a big impact on your child's ability to use the bathroom. If you have chosen to potty train and then switch to a regular bed in the same month, this can be an overwhelming occurrence. It would make sense that your child might have some accidents during this time period. Any tension in the household could also impact the frequency of accidents. If your child is witnessing a lot of arguing and disagreements, this could be another trigger. Just about anything can contribute to the accidents that your child has, so make sure that you are doing your best to keep a stable home environment.

Always approach your child as an empathetic figure in their life. If anything is going on emotionally that is contributing to the accidents, encourage your child to talk to you about it. When you are open with your child, they are going to be more likely to be open in return. Know that asking for help is also okay. If the accidents continue beyond any reason that you can see, consulting your pediatrician is going to be the next step. They will be able to rule out any physical ailments that could be contributing to the accidents, such as UTIs. They will also be able to help you talk to your child to get to the bottom of the reason why the accidents keep happening.

You might notice that your child simply needs more motivation in order to keep using the bathroom. Try to put a rewards system in place if you do not already have one. If you do, think about changing the frequency in which you provide rewards. A simple change like this can lead your child to feel more excited about using the bathroom and staying out of pull-ups. Treat your child as an individual. Do your best not to compare their progress to their friends' or other children their same age. Remember, some children are naturally going to pick up on potty training faster than others.

Why They Happen

There is no concrete answer as to why accidents happen, but it is important that you do not dwell on this question for too long. This will only stress you out, leading you to pass this stressful energy along to your child. They are going to be able to sense when you are unhappy, and they might mistake this feeling for you actually being disappointed with them. Getting to the bottom of why accidents happen can be tough, especially because there are so many factors as to why they can happen. As mentioned, the environment that your child is in can play a big role in whether or not they have bathroom accidents.

Observe your current environment, and make sure you take note of anything that could appear stressful to your child. Even if you do not sense it at first, your child is going to naturally be hyper-aware of these things. Tension is the main issue that can be felt throughout the household. If there are any current disagreements or individuals at odds with one another, do your best to work through these for the sake of harmony. In order for the home environment to be as healthy and loving as possible, all members of it must be willing to get along.

Ask yourself if you are giving your child enough chances to use the bathroom. Having proper access means that your child should be able to go whenever they feel the urge. If they are being put to bed without being given the chance to use the bathroom right before, then it makes sense that accidents will begin to happen. Get into the routine of encouraging your child to use the bathroom right before they go to bed and right after they wake up. This also applies to naps. Whenever you are about to get in the car to go somewhere, encourage your child to use the bathroom, even if they do not feel like they have to go. Getting into these habits at an early age means that they are going to stay with your child as they grow older.

You might be using the wrong tools. If your child has outgrown the children's toilet, but their only option is to use the regular toilet, this can prove to be intimidating. Consider obtaining a potty chair in order to bridge the gap. Your child isn't going to be able to express these things to you, so it is important that you look for the signs on your own. Make sure that the tools you are utilizing make sense for the level that your child is at currently. The same can be said for pull-ups and underwear. By observing your child's progress, you should be able to determine how frequently and when they should be wearing underwear.

Sometimes, accidents will happen for seemingly no reason at all. Potty training is a new skill that your child is learning, and because of this, there should naturally be room for error. Your child must be able to get the hang of a lot of different things in order to successfully be potty trained. It is a new type of skill set that can take some time to form. While it does come naturally to some children, others have a harder time with it. This is why it is so important that you do not compare your child to others that are around the same age. Progress levels are going to vary throughout the entire potty training process.

When you are observant without being reactive, your child is going to be more likely to express any questions or concerns they have to you. Knowing that they have a safe space to discuss these things will truly make a difference in their confidence level. Try to be there for your child as much as you can without completely taking over. While you can take it upon yourself to escort them to the bathroom every few hours and continually ask them if they need to go, it defeats the purpose of what potty training aims to give your child--independence. They are going to need to learn how to recognize these cues on their own, and accidents are going to happen along the way. This is how the point is enforced.

Potty training becomes a life lesson in the sense that your child solely controls the action and the outcome. With this sense of control, they will come to realize that they can change the outcome. Simply going to the bathroom more frequently or being able to better recognize the signs will allow for fewer accidents. It is all one big learning process for both the child and the parent, but it never has to be a stressful one. As long as you are able to remain calm and ready to help, a couple of accidents will simply be a hurdle during the process of potty training, not a sign of regression.

Delays in Progress

Once you get into the process of potty training, you might notice certain points where your child will become delayed. This does not necessarily mean that accidents are to blame; other factors can cause your child to become disinterested in being potty trained, too. One delay stems from having younger siblings. Not all children with younger siblings experience this, but your child might begin to show a desire to use diapers again because they miss the attention that was associated with it. While you are going to be supplementing the attention as you focus on potty training, it is natural for an older child to want to act younger in order to be taken care of again like a younger child. This is very normal, and it can even be seen in cases where the child does not have any younger siblings. If you notice that this is happening, you might need to enforce a better reward system or incorporate more praise when your child uses the bathroom. A little bit of additional motivation will allow your child to see that they are still going to get attention, even after they are successfully potty trained.

Boredom is another thing that can get in the way of continued success. If your child becomes bored with the way that you approach potty training, you need to make sure that you are changing your methods enough to keep them interested. While books on the topic might be enough to intrigue your child at first, they might grow tired of these stories. You can turn your attention to music instead, finding interactive ways for your child to see that potty training is a great thing. Small changes like these will be necessary along the way. Even a pair of new underwear could be enough to get the excitement back. As soon as you notice this boredom, it is important that you make a change. Staying in a rut for too long is going to leave your child in a place where they will start to believe that they do not need to be potty trained.

Aside from these delays that can occur while you are already potty training, consider that developmental delays can also happen. These are things that you cannot control, and they occur naturally depending on your child. If your child isn't walking by the average age, then they likely won't be potty trained by the average age either. Remember that this isn't necessarily a negative thing. If you push your child to start potty training too early, you are only going to be met with frustration and disappointment. Know that it is okay to get a delayed start because children pick up on concepts very quickly. You will be able to move through each step faster because your child is truly ready rather than struggling to accomplish the first one. There is no right or wrong age to begin potty training; only you can decide that for your child.

Mastering the concept of potty training in the home, yet failing to do so in public, is another way that you will notice some delays. It can be difficult because your child might be great at using the toilet in the comfort of your own home, but the idea of using a public toilet can create fear or regression. Public restrooms can be very overwhelming to a child who is new to using the toilet. Whenever possible, try to opt for single bathrooms or family bathrooms. These are more private and usually smaller. They feel like a home bathroom while still being a public option. If you can't find an option like this, try to bring something familiar with you to help your child go in public. Reading a potty training book while on the toilet can remind your child that the concept is still the same.

Health issues can make using the bathroom a painful experience. A lot of children suffer from constipation, and this can be a difficult thing to go through while learning how to use the toilet. Do your best to balance out your child's diet in order to promote a healthy digestive system. Any type of dysfunction with their bowel movements is going to deter them from using the toilet. The same can happen if your child experiences a UTI. While none of these things are entirely preventable, you can ensure that your child practices excellent hygiene and eats a balanced diet in order to promote an easy time on the toilet. Don't let the pain that comes with these health issues keep your child from wanting to continue with potty training. Explaining that these symptoms are normal and that they will go away will reassure your child to keep trying.

Chapter 3
Staying Patient

"Children are like wet cement. Whatever falls on them makes an impression."

-Haim Ginott, child psychologist

While your child is going to be learning many new skills during the process of potty training, you will also be learning simultaneously. Remaining patient while you teach your child is an essential step to a successful potty training experience. All it takes is the loss of your temper to cause your child to lose interest in using the toilet on their own. Remember, fear tactics do not work when it comes to potty training. You cannot threaten to take away privileges because your child is going to be dealing with bodily functions that they do not know how to fully control yet. Getting punished for not using the bathroom or having an accident is a traumatic experience. It becomes very emotionally distressing, and this is exactly what you need to avoid.

The best way for you to exercise your patience is to enter each lesson with a clear state of mind. If you approach your child while you are already feeling stressed out, this will just cause them to feel the same way. View the idea of potty training as a fun and exciting task. If you are not feeling this way, then your doubts are going to become very apparent. Believe in your child and their ability to accomplish this. Know that there is not a child out there who gets the hang of potty training after only one day. It is a lesson that must be taught over several weeks, months, or even years. Also, it can be unpredictable. You might have some really great days followed by a bad one. This is okay; it is normal.

Having fun is highly encouraged when you are potty training! If you can laugh and smile while you are teaching, then you are doing something right. This is also going to keep you in the right mindset to stay patient while brushing off the setbacks. As you learn which techniques work best for your child, you are going to feel confident in your ability as a teacher which is important. When you reach this point, your child is also going to begin feeling more confident. No matter what happens, it happens as a domino effect. If you notice that something isn't working out, accept this and move on to the next method. A lighthearted approach is always going to bring you more success than a strict or rigid one.

Teaching Methods

Depending on your comfort level, teaching your child how to use the bathroom can be done by example. Allowing your child to come into the bathroom with you will take away a lot of the mystery that surrounds potty training. When they learn what using the toilet looks like by having a real-life example in front of them, this will allow them to have the courage to try and do the same thing on their own. As you are in the bathroom, explain what you are doing and why. Having this type of open dialogue with your child will encourage them to ask questions and remain curious about the topic until they are able to master it.

Children respond well to examples. When they can see what is expected of them, it becomes easier to produce the same result. You can read your child as many potty training books as you'd like, but sometimes, a visual example is what it takes to jumpstart their motivation. Stay patient by being willing to answer any questions that your child might have. It is best to go through these things now rather than when they are older and still confused. Your aim is to take away any remaining questions that they might have before they begin using the bathroom on their own.

An alternative method is to place your child on their potty chair or children's toilet and allow them to sit for a few minutes. You do not have to put any pressure on them to use the bathroom, but wait with them and see if anything happens. A lot of the time, children just need a few extra minutes to make something happen. As they are learning how to explore the signs of needing to use the bathroom, it helps them when they are able to just sit on the toilet for a while. This is a very easy-going method because if nothing happens, then it is no big deal. You can simply have your child get dressed and try again in a little while. Though this can be a time-consuming method, it shows your child that you have the patience for the process.

Before your child outgrows their diapers, you can use a cool-sensation brand in order to promote potty training. These diapers are designed to provide your child with a cold, wet feeling when the diaper is dirty. Because of this, most children are going to avoid feeling this way again. You can then introduce the toilet, saying that a way to prevent the above feeling is by using the bathroom. This is a method that works really well for some children. Being able to feel a slight discomfort is all it takes for their potty training skills to kick in. You are likely going to pay more for these diapers, but the transition can be a quick one after your child gets used to them.

One of the most common methods utilized by parents is the interval schedule. By taking your child into the bathroom and encouraging them to go at regular intervals provides a structure as to when to use the toilet. The concept can be confusing to your child at first because using a diaper does not involve a time limit. They are able to go the instant that they feel they have to. Teaching the importance of timing is going to make your potty training transition a lot more successful. Place emphasis on the fact that using the bathroom is encouraged during these intervals, but do not place any pressure on your child. The trick is to stay calm and to offer words of wisdom when you feel that they are needed.

You can incorporate small rewards with any of the methods mentioned above if your child needs a bit more incentive. Offering something like a sticker can motivate your child to use the bathroom. Make sure that you keep the reward fairly small when you are giving one every time your child uses the bathroom. You can provide a bigger reward when your child poops in the toilet because this is a little bit harder to accomplish than urination. Otherwise, make sure that you keep the rewards system reasonable. The idea is that you will eventually need to wean your child off of these rewards because they will be using the toilet on their own with no further incentive. If the prize is too great, then they will continue to expect it even as they grow older.

No matter which method you choose, even if it is one of your own, you will need to pick the one that your child responds best to. No child is exactly alike, so you might have to experiment with different ones until you find something that truly motivates them to want to use the bathroom. Potty training does not have to be as rigid and meticulous as you expect; you can incorporate fun into it! When you make it fun and exciting, you will find that your child will probably respond better to the training.

Fun Games

- Magic Potty: A few drops of food coloring are all it takes for this game. Place some blue coloring into your child's toilet, or the big toilet, and watch their look of amazement as the water turns green after they urinate. Your child will associate urination as the "magic" behind this game, and seeing the color change will motivate them to do it again. You can utilize this game when your child needs some extra motivation to use the bathroom.

- Eye Spy: As your child is sitting on the toilet, sit near them and encourage them to take a look around at all of the different objects that they can see from where they are sitting. Tell them to silently pick one, and then use your time in the bathroom to "spy" what object they have found while they use the bathroom. This is a great way to pass the time and it keeps potty training interesting.

- Singing: Sing a song with your child as they sit on the toilet. Normally, this allows them to become comfortable enough to use the bathroom because it relaxes them. If you need more time, you can hum songs to one another and guess what they are. A bonus option is to teach your child songs about using the bathroom. There are plenty of resources available, and this will allow your child to feel even more comfortable with the process of using the toilet.

- Bubbles: Blowing bubbles can actually stimulate your child's abdominal muscles enough to allow them to use the bathroom. Once they are on the toilet, give them a bottle of bubbles for a few minutes. This is going to be very fun to your child while also providing them with an easier way to use the bathroom. You can keep the bottle in the bathroom so that your child associates blowing bubbles with being on the toilet.

- Chucking Diapers: This game is a more symbolic one. With the remainder of the diapers you have, allow your child to see them and explain that you won't need them anymore because they are going to be using the toilet. Place a basket into a large, open space and allow your child to throw as many diapers as they can into the basket. This serves as a way for your child to part with their diapers and accept that potty training is the next step.

- Charting: As you are training your child, you want to promote the idea that going to the bathroom is a natural occurrence. Make a chart with every household member's name on it, pets included! Allow your child to mark an X next to the name after each member of the family uses the bathroom. Your child is going to want their name to have an X next to it, too. It is a fun and informative way to teach them that using the bathroom is something that is done multiple times each day by everyone in the house.

- Toy Training: After you have taught your child the basics of potty training, encourage them to teach one of their toys how to do the same thing. Working step-by-step with their toy is going to allow them to remember all of the things that you have taught them. When put in the role of a teacher, it is natural for children to want to "impress" their student. Most children really enjoy the idea that they can be the one in charge of teaching.

- Decoration: Give your child a pack of stickers. Allow them to decorate their potty chair or their children's toilet. It is a fun way to customize something that your child should see as theirs. When they feel that they have ownership of an item, it is more likely that they are going to want to utilize it. As your child progresses with their potty training, you can give them more stickers to continue decorating.

- Aiming: This is a game that is geared toward little boys who are learning how to stand and urinate. Throw a few Cheerios into the toilet and allow your child to aim at them. This is a great game because explaining how to aim can be very difficult if your child isn't provided with some further instructions. The concept of this game is simple enough to be fun, but helpful enough to improve their ability to aim.

- Scented Soaps: Washing your hands comes after using the bathroom, as your child should know. Encourage them to use the toilet and then allow them to use a scented soap to wash their hands with. Once they get the hang of using the toilet, you can allow them to pick out their own scents that are used especially for times when they successfully use the bathroom.

Reward System

We have touched on the topic of having a reward system, and you will realize that there are many ways that you can implement one. It is best if you have the system planned out before you begin rewarding your child. This will eliminate any confusion or misuse of the system. For example, if you give in and allow your child to have a reward even if they do not use the bathroom, this is only going to send them mixed signals. They will see potty training as something that is optional, not a necessity. The main rule that you should follow is to only provide a reward when your child actually uses the bathroom.

By reinforcing their behavior, your child is going to learn that going to the bathroom is a positive action. Though they will know this naturally, it does help to have a little bit of encouragement. This is why punishment is not recommended when it comes to accidents or refusal to use the bathroom; the pressure is only going to scare your child and discourage any progress that you have made. Only use positive reinforcement and use it well. The reward system is supposed to be exciting to your child, and it also displays a sense of support. When you are reinforcing their behavior, they will take that as a message to continue.

The frequency is up to you. Think about what will really work best with your schedule. Are you going to be at home while you potty train? Do you think you might go out and use a public restroom with your child? Sometimes, it can be hard to provide a reward if you are not prepared. For example, maybe you did not bring one with you when you went out to run errands. This is something to consider when you are setting up your reward schedule. Make sure that you can follow through with giving the reward each time that you agree to do so.

Providing a reward after each time your child uses the bathroom is very encouraging in the beginning. Consider tapering this down to once a day and then once a week. The idea is that you are going to keep your child interested in potty training by using the rewards but not being dependent on the rewards. You will need your child to know that getting rewarded is something special that happens when they are first learning. As they grow older, they should be able to find their own incentive.

You can observe how your child is responding to the reward system before you decide to taper it down. If getting prizes every day is making a huge difference in the frequency of your child's ability to use the bathroom, then keep this schedule for a few weeks. As time goes on, explain to your child that they are doing such a great job they will actually be getting different prizes. You can then switch the frequency to once a week. Since the reward is new, your child should not feel any less excited about the change in schedule.

In general, the reward should be something fairly small. Stickers and mini toys are normally what parents like to give to their children. These rewards must be something that you are able to obtain in bulk. If you allow your child to get a brand-new big toy each time they use the bathroom, you are going to be training them in a counter-productive way that is going to cost you a fortune. This is why it is essential to be mindful of the prizes that you choose.

A reward system should be used as a supplemental form of encouragement. While it is a very exciting perk about learning how to use the bathroom, it is not the only one. Remember, you should still be allowing your child to discover that using the bathroom and gaining this independence is a big step in life. It is one that is exciting on its own and necessary to get the hang of. Answer all of their questions and check-in with them frequently about any concerns they might be having. An open line of communication is the key to becoming great at potty training.

Chapter 4
What Not to Do

"Children need models rather than critics."

-Joseph Joubert, French moralist

Much like all areas of parenting, you probably wish that there were clear-cut guidelines for potty training. With the individuality of each child and the level that they are going to progress, it can be difficult to say what should be done. Potty training is most successful when different methods are tried and your child's ability to grasp the concept is carefully monitored. There are a few tips that you can hold on to, however. These are some of the things that you should avoid during your potty training process, no matter how old or how experienced your child is.

The below methods are sometimes used when the parent feels that there is no other choice. Remember, patience is a huge part of potty training on your own behalf. Your child is going to experience many victories but also many setbacks throughout the process. It is important to avoid these methods because they can actually cause your child to regress or to become disinterested in using the bathroom on their own. Fear tactics and threats are not the way to encourage potty training. You should only promote behaviors that uplift your child.

Scolding and Punishment

After receiving a punishment, your child naturally becomes fearful. Whether the fear lasts for a few seconds or a lifetime, this is something that impacts your child's ability to learn. When fear takes over the brain, it becomes the main focus. Even if your child knows exactly what needs to be done, they might begin to second-guess themselves after being punished for not using the bathroom (or for having an accident). In this way, scolding or punishing your child can backfire when it comes to the progress that you have made. It can be challenging to get your child to a place where they no longer feel this fear.

Aside from developing a fear of using the bathroom, punishing your child for these reasons can also strain your relationship. While punishment is a necessary disciplinary action, sometimes they cause more damages than helping a parent when it comes to potty training. Because you are going to be continually helping your child use the bathroom, you need to have a trusting relationship in the process. Even if the punishment isn't long-lasting, its impact might be. Children choose to hold on to certain things that you might not even realize they are holding on to. Along with halting any potty training progress, this can also cause your child to become fearful of future new situations.

Overall, it just makes sense to skip out on the punishment when you are potty training your child. While it can be an incredibly frustrating job for both of you, remember that each child is going to develop the skills eventually. It is a natural instinct that needs time to develop. When you punish your child for not learning this fast enough, it causes them to feel humiliated. Imaginably, this can also impact your child's future learning abilities. They are likely going to want to give up if they don't get it right the first time in fear of being scolded or punished.

A distressed child is one who is more likely to have accidents. This is another way that punishment can backfire while you are potty training. It becomes a never-ending cycle of showing your disappointment and your child feeling intimidated by it. The trick is to let your child know that potty training is possible for all people and ages. By sending a message that it is only a "big girl" or "big boy" responsibility, this can also place the wrong kind of pressure on them. Take away all of the intimidating aspects that you can. This will help your child feel as though they can accomplish it on their own.

By avoiding punishment, you are taking all of the stress out of the process of potty training. Many parents don't realize this until it is too late and they have already tried using punishments. A stress-free environment is not only a great thing for potty training but also for the entire household. When you are holding on to that type of tension, it can easily become contagious. Even if you are trying to hide it, your child is likely going to be able to sense it from you.

If you are finding it difficult to potty train without punishment, then you need to make sure that your own mood and feelings are in check. Do not try to work with your child if you are in a bad mood, regardless of what is causing you stress. You are going to be more likely to snap or punish your child, and this is only going to send the wrong messages, as you know. Try to remain in the most uplifted mood that you can each time that you begin potty training. The experience is supposed to be fun and exciting, so it is important that you have a demeanor to match.

This is a time that you are only going to experience with your child once, and it is a milestone. No matter how many ups and downs you encounter, you should be able to look back on the experience once it is over and remember all of the positive aspects of potty training. Make sure to take breaks when necessary in order to keep harmony in the environment. If there is another parent in the household or someone else who can help, try to take turns with teaching. Having a few different teaching styles can help your child while also helping the parental figures stay calm and relaxed.

If you are still unsure about whether or not to punish your child, remember this – a punishment should only occur when your child knowingly does something wrong. Having an accident while potty training does not qualify, nor does being not able to use the bathroom in the given moment. These are all bodily functions that your child is still trying their best to figure out, so you must do your best to support them through this process. Save the punishment for times when you do need to enforce more respect in the parent/child relationship. When it comes to potty training, your child already knows that you are very knowledgeable about the topic. They are going to respect this knowledge, and as they become ready to use the bathroom on their own, they are going to start asking you more questions.

Denial of Drinks

Some parents believe that eliminating liquids from the child's diet during certain periods of time can actually help with potty training. Not only is this untrue, but it also can cause your child to regress much like being punished does. By denying your child the request to drink something, this is already coming from a punishment type of approach. Because your child has done nothing wrong to deserve it, they are going to be confused and might start lashing out in the process. While it might seem logical and helpful to cut down on the amount of liquid that your child is drinking because you want to assist them with the accidents that they are having, it just isn't a practical or long-term solution.

Nighttime can be the worst time for a newly potty-trained child. It is the time that they are going to have to hold it the longest if they are not able to get up and use the bathroom on their own at night. Having a lot to drink before bed is naturally going to mean that your child will have to use the bathroom more frequently for the next several hours. Instead of cutting down on or eliminating drinks during this time, make a plan for what your child needs to do if they must get up to use the bathroom. If your child feels prepared, this is going to make nighttime a lot more peaceful.

Another option is to teach the child to get out of the bed and wake up a parent for assistance with using the bathroom at night. Of course, this means that you will continually have to get up and help your child throughout the night, but it could be a quick way to teach them that they can use the bathroom if necessary in order to avoid wetting the bed. When you choose to go with this method, your child will likely pick up on the idea quickly. This means that you should only have to remain on-call for a short period of time until they feel comfortable. Make sure that the bathroom is well lit by nightlights and that any potty chair or other device is set up and ready to use. This will make your child's experience one that seems more suitable to tackle alone.

We recommend using pull-ups frequently when your child needs to go for an extended period of time without using the bathroom. This can be a good solution for when you are in the car and you do not have the option to stop. Your child is likely going to be eating and drinking in the car, and this means that they are highly likely to need to use the bathroom. If you feel that they aren't going to be able to hold it during the whole duration of the car ride, then opting for pull-ups is going to be a smart move in this case. You must play it by ear as to what you feel your child is ready for.

Dehydration is also something to pay attention to. Your child's urine is going to be noticeably darker in color if they don't consume fluids properly. The urine becomes very yellow and might have a distinct smell. Staying hydrated keeps your child's bathroom usage regular, and it allows for proper digestion. All of this can impact their overall immune system and ability to have enough energy to get through the day. If you were to deny them drinks, you would also be sacrificing certain aspects of their health. For the possibility to avoid a few accidents, it makes sense to simply seek out another method rather than one that is going to cause additional problems.

Given all of the alternative options, you can see that denying your child drinks at any given point does not make any sense. Potty training comes with a sense of innovation--you must always be testing out new methods. Sometimes, it can take a combination of a lot of different ways. No matter which approach you consider, your child is going to respond best to the one that allows for maximum comfort and self-confidence building. Try to empower them as best as you can, giving them all of the courage necessary to truly feel that potty training is a task that can be mastered.

Pressure to Start

Much like anything else in life, the pressure to perform is one that can hinder progress. If you have ever experienced excitement about something, all it takes is a push from someone with more experience to make you question your own abilities. This is how your child feels when you push the idea of potty training. It is one thing to build up excitement about the process because it is a very exciting time in any child's life, but a nagging push to start potty training isn't going to automatically make your child want to learn. Your patience needs to be under control from the very beginning, even before you start teaching.

How do you make sure that you aren't being too pushy, yet being informative enough to answer all of your child's questions? The best way to determine this is to listen to the way that your child talks about the subject. Remember that curiosity is a great sign! When your child is curious, this means that they have thought in-depth about the idea of potty training. If you notice that your child is at this stage, do your best to bring it up in conversation regularly. Explain how one day they are going to be using the bathroom too. Make sure that you keep each talk that you have lighthearted.

When enough curiosity is displayed, this is normally when you will notice some of the signs that were discussed that indicate your child is ready for potty training. This is generally how the pattern forms, but know that this isn't the only way. If your child has a fear of potty training, as a lot of children do because they feel intimidated, make sure that you take this fear away as best as you can. Show them the tools that can help them in order to make the experience less scary. If you pressure your child while fear is already present, this is only going to cause even more resistance.

No mention of potty training does not necessarily equate to no interest. Your child might simply grasp the concept and feel content with it, despite having no outward interest in potty training. This is also a great sign, but it can be harder to realize how your child is feeling when they don't express it to you. To gauge your child's interest level, you can try bringing up the topic. Again, keeping it lighthearted is always going to be the best approach. To stir up some excitement, you can try some of the fun game ideas that were mentioned in the previous chapter. This is enough to make potty training seem interesting while also keeping the pressure to a minimum.

One of the worst things that can happen from pressuring your child to potty train before they are fully ready is a regression. This can occur at any age and any level of potty training experience. Whether you have been working on it for 1 week or 1 year, too much pressure on your child can lead them to revert to using diapers or having lots of accidents. This can be a very frustrating time for you both, but it is essential to still keep the pressure off of your child. If they are already feeling uncertain, a method that involves bullying isn't going to allow them to see how easy and fun potty training is. They will need to see this for themselves with the help of the tools and methods that you use.

Regression is one of the main fears that the parent will have when embarking on the potty training journey. Let go of this fear and pay attention to your child's level of progress. Because there can be no true comparison between ages and experience levels, you just need to work based on the information that you see in front of you. Sometimes, your child just isn't going to be ready, and that is okay. As mentioned, you can simply wait a few more months and then try again. Regression doesn't happen out of nowhere. It is something that is absolutely triggered, whether it be situational, environmental, or personal. By remaining confident in your child, you aren't leaving any room for these regressive behaviors to form.

Many parents believe in the idea of no formal potty training. This means that they allow their children to become curious about using the bathroom whenever it happens, and then they help them do so when asked. There is no preparation or setup because this method revolves around the child's natural inclination to potty train themselves. This is a way to truly guarantee that you aren't pressuring your child to do anything that they aren't ready for. It allows them to be in control of their bodies and their life changes, an interesting approach. No matter what, all children are going to reach a point in life where the idea of potty training becomes of interest.

The following are some tips that you can follow to ensure that you are doing your best to be a great support system and teacher:

- Let Your Child Talk: When you let them do the talking, they are going to be able to tell you exactly how they feel. By prompting your child with certain questions and answers, you are planting ideas into their head of how they *think* you want them to answer. All honest conversations with children are best done when they begin them.

- Keep Everything Lighthearted: A topic that is touched on frequently because it is so important--make sure that your child can sense that you have a lighthearted mood surrounding the topic of potty training. If you are feeling too high strung or frustrated to handle the task, your child might begin to believe that they are causing this problem. This is when the fear and insecurity can set in.

- Get Rid of Comparison: Whether you are worried that your child isn't "on track" or you are wondering what other children of the same age are doing, it is best to leave comparison out of potty training altogether. This allows you both to have a stress-free experience at your own pace, which is what matters most. The instant that you imply that your child is being compared to other children, this can definitely lead to insecurity that will halt all progress. Potty training is not a competition, so there is no need to make sure that your child is doing the same thing as any other child is doing.

Chapter 5
How to Talk to Your Child

"The best way to make children good is to make them happy."

-Oscar Wilde, author and poet

Communication is essential for a successful potty training experience. Not only do you have to clearly communicate to your child the process of using the bathroom and what the cues feel like, but they also must be able to communicate with you in return. They are going to have to tell you when they think they need to use the bathroom, or when they have had an accident. This openness is what makes for the most positive experience, no matter what is going on. It can be difficult for some parents to talk to their children about using the bathroom. For one, it is a personal topic. It can also be hard to bring the subject up for both the parent and the child.

Making sure that you are clear with your child is going to teach them that they can ask you about these things. When you talk to them as you would another adult about the process of using the bathroom, they are going to feel respected and important. There is no need to make up names for the different actions that can take place on a toilet. Explain them clearly to your child so that they know what to expect. If you talk to your child by working around the actual topic, they are only going to be confused once it comes time for potty training.

Bring up all of the great things that come from becoming potty trained. You can mention the fact that your child gets to pick out their own underwear or the reward system (if you choose to use one). There are plenty of positive things that you can mention in order to encourage your child. Try not to make the downsides seem too scary or difficult to overcome. Other than explaining that accidents are normal, you likely won't have to deal with many other negatives unless they come up as your child is learning. This step-by-step approach with clear communication is a guarantee that you will be giving your child the best experience that you can.

Banishing Baby Talk

Because potty training is such a milestone, you will want to ensure that you are sending a message to your child that says you believe in them. Talking to your child in a baby voice is probably something that you have done for their whole life, as it is with most parents. When you speak to a child this way, it actually enforces the message that you see them as a baby. The independence and confidence that is needed are not going to come if the child still feels like a baby. They are going to be more likely to feel like they can stay in diapers longer.

It can be hard to form reasonable boundaries between yourself and your child, especially when you strive to have a relationship that has excellent communication. Talking in a baby voice to your child sets a boundary that you don't necessarily want with potty training. It suggests that you do not wish to communicate on a deeper level. Your child is going to need this connection as they work on becoming potty trained. It is a big step for all children, and it can be hard to remember this as the parent.

Think about the boundary that you set with your child as one that can expand with time. The older they get, the more that you are going to trust them. Show them that you have respect for them by patiently explaining the answers to any questions they have and maintaining proper eye contact. Potty training can truly be a trust-building activity. You can still show kindness without dropping your level of communication down to baby talk. Use your eye contact, tone, and body language to express this.

You'll notice that your child will likely start to feel proud when you start talking to them about important things. It allows for a sense of emotional growth, and this is important as your child goes through the various changes that life brings. This is a great time for bonding on a level that you might not have reached yet. Don't second guess your child's ability to understand you because you'll never know until you try this approach.

An example in today's society that you can use is the children's show, *Blues Clues*. The host, Steve, never uses baby talk. He works with the children through various adventures by guiding them with a gentle yet wise tone. This is the exact approach that works well when you are potty training. It is mature enough to be respected and kind enough to not be intimidating. The next time that you decide to have a conversation with your child about potty training, be mindful about the way that you are speaking.

The following are some tips that you can use when you are adjusting the way that you talk to your child:

- Make Sure the Household is on Board: When you are aiming to shift away from baby talk, it makes sense that everyone else in the household abides by this rule, too. It also makes the difference a lot more noticeable, and your child is going to be able to pick up on the fact that the whole family considers them a big boy or big girl.

- Provide Corrections: Just because you stop using baby talk does not mean that your child will right away. If you notice that your child is mispronouncing words or saying things that are along the lines of baby talk, correct them. You can still be kind and gentle when you do this, but it will get your child into the habit of speaking correctly.

- Ask About Their Ideas: A great way to encourage your child to use their voice is by prompting them to talk about their thoughts and ideas. When they explain things that they are passionate about, they are less likely to use baby talk. Allow them several opportunities to talk to you in this way. These "brainstorming" sessions are going to be great for your child's development and maturity.

● Talk About Your Day: Telling your child about your day in your regular voice will show them that they can do the same with you. When you can have this type of dialogue together, you'll find that your bond will become even stronger. This is a point in your child's life when you will get to know all of the traits of their personality and the person that they are becoming.

When you stop allowing baby talk in your home, you are helping your child grow as well as preparing them for their potty training journey. It does not mean you are being harsh or too critical because there comes a point in every child's life when they must learn how to properly express themselves. Your child will be able to fully express how they are feeling and if they need to use the bathroom, which is going to make your role a lot easier. Instead of guessing if they are about to have an accident or if they are scared to use the bathroom alone, they will be able to just let you know themselves.

Explaining the Process

Again, it is natural that you have certain boundaries with your children. This is normal for all parents. There comes a point in time where it is helpful to let go of certain boundaries. When you are explaining the process of what happens when you use the bathroom and how to pay attention to cues that the body gives you, it is crucial to explain this to your child in detail. When they know what to expect, it takes away a lot of the fear or wonder involved with potty training. During this age is a great time to be reviewing facts on different body parts and what they do.

Talk about the body using the proper terms. This doesn't need to be a complicated lesson, but make it accurate enough for your child to be able to understand everything. It is best to utilize the correct terminology in order to avoid any further confusion. Your child will be able to grasp these concepts better than you expect. When you talk to them in a mature fashion, they will likely respond in the same way. Bring the topic up frequently, and let your child ask questions. This is going to be the start of the openness that is necessary for having an easy time with potty training. Don't hesitate to check-in with your child every so often to make sure that they understand everything that is going on with their anatomy.

You can teach your child about the digestion process or give a small review if this is something that they already know. Also, go over the fact that there are two ways to use the bathroom--going pee and poop. Explain how the pressure feels different based on which way your child needs to use the bathroom. There is also a chance that you are going to encounter the topics of diarrhea or constipation. Make sure that you allow your child to learn from the very beginning that these things happen sometimes, and they should not be worried.

Talk about wiping correctly, especially for little girls. Wiping back to front can cause problems that are painful to deal with, so it is important that you explain this to your child in detail. The amount of toilet paper to be used is also something that you need to go over. Children can easily accidentally clog the toilet because they are unaware that using too much toilet paper is a bad thing. Explain that nothing else ever needs to be flushed down there except for pee, poop, and toilet paper. This will save you a lot of frustration in the future.

Discuss the topic of germs and why handwashing is very important. Teaching your child about the various bacteria that exist if they do not wash their hands provides them with an incentive to make sure that they do not forget. Once you get your child gets into the habit of having great hygiene, it is normally something that stays with them for life. Not only is hand washing the right thing to do because of the germs, but it also allows your children to think about the other people that they interact with and how it serves as a common courtesy. Explain how they probably wouldn't want to play with another kid who didn't wash their hands, and the other kid would likely feel the same way. This keeps the topic lighthearted yet important.

Talk about the differences between diapers, pull-ups, and underwear. Explain that babies wear diapers before they know how to walk and talk because this is the only way that they are able to use the bathroom. You can then move on to the fact that older children can use the bathroom, but they might need a little bit of help as they are getting used to this. You don't need to make pull-ups sound like a negative thing, especially if your child might have to utilize them while they are getting used to being potty trained.

Of course, you will want to make the option of wearing and selecting underwear to be the most exciting. Explain that if your child is able to keep their underwear dry, they will be able to pick out some new pairs. This can prove to be very exciting to a child who is new to wearing underwear. With all of the different designs and cartoon characters available, they will have a blast deciding which pair that they want to wear each day. This is one of the most fun aspects of potty training that will definitely keep your child engaged if you can explain the process from the beginning. It is worth a mention each time that you notice they are losing interest in becoming potty trained.

Mentioning the Positives

When teaching your child anything new, it is helpful if you consider a list of all the positive things that you can say about this topic. Your child is going to be much more responsive to the training of any kind when you can display an enthusiastic attitude toward the learning experience. Consider these positive benefits of potty training when you feel that you need to boost your child's morale:

- Confidence Boost: Your child is going to feel on top of the world when they master the art of being potty trained. With all of the new information that they are going to learn, plus the new underwear that they will get to wear, this is going to make your child feel super special and important. This is a great thing to celebrate! Allow them to feel happy and confident that they are able to use the bathroom on their own. It is a milestone that only happens once in their life, so it is right to make sure that you congratulate them once they have the routine down.

- Becoming Independent: You know very well that as your child grows older, they are going to become more independent. They might not realize this, however, believing that they are only going to have minimal control of what goes on in their own lives. Show your child that independence can be a great thing. Having the freedom of choice to use the bathroom when they need to and wear the underwear that they love is a great feeling. Allow your child to know that this is what it means to be independent and that it doesn't always have to be hard or scary. This is the type of mindset that shows your child how to navigate through the rest of the world.

- Nature's Way: Let your child know that using the bathroom is a completely positive and natural action. Not only do humans partake, but animals also need to relieve themselves. For a child who is around 2 years old, the mention of different animals is likely going to be intriguing. They are going to want to hear more about this, and you can turn nature into a very positive experience that is meant to make your child even more comfortable. Try to eliminate anything that makes your child feel that they are doing something wrong by going through the process of potty training, especially if they begin to have accidents.

● Sense of Awareness: When your child uses the bathroom, they are automatically going to become more self-aware. This is important to any young person's life in terms of developmental traits. Explain to your child the importance of being aware of their own actions as well as exercising their free will. It is also a great lesson on responsibility, showcasing that if they do not get to the bathroom in time, they are going to have an accident. Again, without scaring them, simply explain the different possibilities while encouraging your child to think for themselves and to take action accordingly.

While these are some great examples of the things that you can mention to your child in order to encourage their progress, it is also essential that you keep yourself motivated. You are going to need a confidence boost as well, especially during the more challenging times when potty training. Remind yourself that you are doing this in your child's best interest. Assuming they have displayed proper signs of being ready to use the bathroom, you are providing them with the information that they need in order to turn their instincts into a reality.

With your guidance, you are allowing your child to reach a milestone. This is one that brings a sense of great importance into their life while teaching you that the baby stage does not last forever. It is likely that you are going to cherish the moments of changing diapers by way of a distant memory. Your child's newfound happiness and skills are going to outweigh the days when you had to bring a diaper bag with you at all times. Think about all of the money that you will be saving as soon as you eliminate diapers and pull-ups. There will be no more need for single-use items that are messy and can be inconvenient. Your child is going to be able to use the bathroom with only a little bit of assistance to start out with.

The amount of time that you spend planning and preparing to go anywhere, even just to the grocery store, gets cut in half when you have a potty-trained child. You probably don't even realize how much time you spend on this aspect of life, but you will when your child is able to use the bathroom on their own. Instead of packing bags of supplies, diapers, and changes of clothes, you will be able to focus on the tasks at hand. Your child will become a more active part of your life, realizing that they are able to make decisions on their own and take care of themselves in a small sense. It is another moment that happens so fast that you might not even realize it is happening. Potty training is full of various positive elements for both yourself and your child to experience together.

Chapter 6
Transitional Stages

"Children are not things to be molded, but are people to be unfolded."

-Jess Lair, author

As much as parents would love for it to happen this way, potty training never happens overnight. It is an ongoing process that must be worked on every single day if you want to see a noticeable improvement. It sounds like an intimidating task, but just remember that you are teaching your child how to do something that already comes naturally to them--try not to overthink this. Be aware that your child might need to spend some time in a transitional stage of potty training before you can officially consider them potty trained. Never feel ashamed or embarrassed for having to utilize one of these steps--it is very normal.

There are some things that you must do as a parent in order to allow your child to thrive. Think about potty training transitional stages as one of these things. From knowing when to safely make the switch to underwear to successfully making it through the night without an accident, you are going to be guiding your child through a lot of changes. Of course, you will want to make this as easy for them as you can. If there is anything that you can do for your child, you would likely do it in a heartbeat. Before you get deep into a potty training routine, consider which transitional steps you can use to fill in any gaps that might appear. Your child might need the extra push in order to succeed.

Utilizing a transitional stage does not mean that you are not doing a good job of teaching your child. Some children are just going to need more help than others. Do not take one of these stages as a personal attack on your ability to teach your child. Learn how to utilize these stages for the benefits that they contain. Be proud of yourself for thinking about this aspect ahead of time, never letting your child know that there is not a plan. It is important that you keep the environment as controlled and relaxed as you can. This is going to promote more bathroom usage.

Diapers and Underwear

The individual actions of wearing diapers and underwear have likely already been discussed with your child, but there are times when you will realize that they are just not ready to make the switch. A great way that you can introduce the underwear is by placing a pair over your child's diaper. This is a way to keep the underwear clean while also allowing your child to feel as though they are really wearing it. While it is a simple trick that you can utilize, it does a lot to boost your child's interest in wanting to wear more underwear. Let them know that the diaper or pull-up is not meant to stay on with the underwear forever; teach them that this is a temporary thing.

While it seems that you are tricking your child by utilizing this method, you are actually just being honest. By letting them know that the underwear is supposed to be worn alone, your child is going to pick up on the fact that you are using the diaper as a safety net. They might even become so motivated that they feel like they want to show you they can wear the underwear on its own. This determination is what gets children to hold their urge to use the bathroom for the sake of not wanting to mess up their underwear and because they want to impress the parent. While you are going to be proud no matter what, make sure that you take extra care to express your pride in your child when they are able to wear underwear on its own.

It is likely that you won't have to use this method for very long. The excitement that it creates for your child is usually enough to promote a much higher interest in wearing underwear. Even if you do stick with it for some time, it is not a negative thing. It also isn't adding any additional time to your schedule. Because it stays clean, you won't have to worry about frequent washing if your child does happen to use their diaper. The main thing to remember is that it is a transitional type of method, so no matter what happens, it is not going to become a permanent habit in your child's potty training regimen.

You can apply the same concept while using pull-ups. This is when your child is very close to being able to stay dry, but they might require the safety of pull-ups for a little while longer. Underwear will be able to fit over these, as well. Give this option to your child and see if it provides them with the confidence to believe that they are able to wear the underwear on its own. No matter what your child prefers, support their decision. Much like starting potty training, there is no specific time that they must wear underwear. The timeline is going to be individual to your child's needs.

Underwear does not need to be used as a bribe or a prize. Never use your child's status as an indication of how well they are doing with their potty training. If you start to do this, they are going to feel pressured into thinking that they need to be wearing underwear sooner. Being able to wear it and stay dry is an individual accomplishment that your child will reach when they are ready. As a parent, you must believe in this. Any doubts or worries can potentially be taken as disappointment by your child, so try to remain as easy going as you can on the topic.

As soon as your child begins to ask for an underwear, allow them to wear it. You can test their ability to hold their bladder by letting them wear it without too much additional preparation. The best time to let them wear it is when they have the most interest in it on their own accord. If accidents start to happen, you will learn what transitional methods you might have to begin with before they can try wearing it again on their own. This trial run is going to be an experiment, so make sure that you do not hold too much weight to it. Again, don't let your child feel as though you are disappointed with them if they do have accidents at first. This is only going to get better the more that they learn how to control their urge to go.

While diapers help keep a child comfortable before they are fully ready to become potty trained, you will want to make sure that they do not form an attachment to them in the same way that they do with underwear. If they get too used to diapers, it makes sense that they might not want to stop using them. This is why it is essential to make potty training seem exciting and intriguing. You will want to do the same thing with underwear. Teach your child that diapers are used for a designated amount of time and that being able to wear underwear is special. As your child grows, they are often going to gravitate toward things that make them feel big and important.

Nighttime

The most daunting time for parents and children alike who are new to potty training os nighttime. It can create difficulties. Because your child is normally asleep for at least 8-10 hours each night, maybe more, this is when they must hold their urge to go for the longest. From the very beginning, allow your child to realize that they can get out of bed to use the bathroom if they need to. While this appears to be common sense, it likely goes against bedtime rules that you have set for your child from early on. Getting out of bed after being tucked in can seem almost taboo to a child, but allowing them to realize that using the bathroom is a necessity will highlight its importance.

While you want your child to feel free to get up if they need to, you will simultaneously want to make sure that you are giving them many chances to use the bathroom before you tuck them in. Remind them to go after dinner and after any bedtime activities. Right before they get into bed, check-in again and ask if they might need to go. After some time, you will no longer have to ask because the process becomes a habit. This is a habit that will greatly benefit your child as they become more familiar with potty training. It provides them with the exact independence that they need in order to take care of themselves.

Night lights make the process of using the bathroom after bedtime a lot less scary. Make sure that the toilet is lit adequately in order to prevent any fears from keeping your child in bed and having an accident. You can even place night lights in the halls and your child's bedroom if they aren't there already to make the path to the toilet clear. Let your child help you pick out a bathroom night light so that they feel connected to it in some way. It is a small thing that you can do to involve them in the process of using the bathroom at night, further proving that the experience does not have to be scary. They will likely be thrilled at the idea of being able to make a choice.

The same thought process can be put behind which underwear your child wears to bed. Allow them to pick out their own pair so that they feel a status of importance. Nighttime is a time when children tend to become vulnerable, possibly reverting back into their younger ways. Choosing underwear to sleep in will remind them that they are taking a step toward becoming more independent. While it does imply that there is some responsibility here, it also brings a fun aspect to the process. Their entire nighttime routine will become something that they look forward to, possibly even promoting them to want to get to bed sooner. Overall, it brings a lot of positive aspects to your nightly experience.

Get everything in the bathroom ready ahead of time. Even if your child does not need to get up at all during the night, it is still a good idea to be prepared. If they have everything that they need, then it is less likely that they are going to need to wake you up for help. If a potty chair is being used, fasten it to the toilet securely before you go to bed. Make sure that there is plenty of toilet paper to use, replacing any empty rolls. If your child needs a step stool in order to wash their hands, put it out in front of the sink for ease of access. An additional option is to keep a pair of clean underwear out for your child in case an accident does occur. They will be able to put their dirty underwear in the hamper while changing into a dry pair and then getting back into bed.

While there are plenty of things that you can do to help your child just in case they need to get up at night, remember that it is not a guarantee. They might have everything that they need in abundance, but their lack of confidence might still cause them to have an accident or wake you up for help. Know that this is also a temporary transitional stage that you must work through before your child becomes fully potty trained and self-sufficient. As long as you are doing your best to take away the fear of using the bathroom alone at night, then you are doing everything you can for your child. They will become more comfortable with the idea the more that they experience it.

If you have to use pull-ups at nighttime, you can incorporate a sense of independence in your children by allowing them to change themselves when they wake up. Show them how to discard the pull-ups and teach them that they can put on their own clean pair of underwear. Even if they need to use the pull-ups during the night, they will still be practicing their independence by cleaning up after themselves and getting into their underwear. It is a way to further improve on the potty training process while still utilizing a transitional stage.

Travel

Whether you are taking a long trip or just going to the store, you will need to take your child's bladder into account. Children are quick to pick up on the concepts of potty training, but being able to put them into effect outside of the home can often become a challenge. This does not mean that your child isn't learning quickly enough, but it does mean that it might take some additional mastering before your child can stay dry while you travel. Much like any other step, patience is required here. Before you plan on going anywhere, add a few additional minutes before you step out the door to remind your child to try to use the bathroom. Explain that you are going out, and there isn't going to be an option to use the bathroom while you are riding in the car.

Even if your child is no longer using diapers or pull-ups, it is still a good idea to at least bring a clean pair of underwear with you and a change of clothes in the car. If an accident does occur, it takes less time to get your child into dry clothes than trying to dry their current outfit while making sure that they are clean. This is something that you should start doing out of habit for the first few months that they begin wearing underwear. The more you take them places and the more that you notice they are staying dry, you less you'll have to worry about this step.

As discussed earlier, public restroom options can be very intimidating to a child. Because there is so much accessibility, your child might feel too shy to use the bathroom when other people are coming in and out of the room. For the first few months to years, you are probably going to have to go inside the stall with your child. You can provide distractions to help your child go without paying attention to what is going on outside of the stall. Singing or humming songs can be a great game to play that will also provide an adequate distraction. Your aim should be to help your child feel as comfortable as they do when they are using their own toilet. Even to an adult, you know how intimidating the process can be.

Other than this, there isn't much else that you can do to prepare your child for using the bathroom while you are on the go. The concepts all stay the same, as they should. You should not over-complicate the situation or else your child will feel intimidated before they even try to use the bathroom. Leading by example works well for this. Allow your child to come into the stall with you and use the bathroom first. Sometimes, this is all it takes to encourage them to want to go too. Luckily, a lot of public places do have larger stalls meant for parents with children or even private family restroom options. Keep an eye out for these when you can.

Timing is everything when you are traveling. Your child might be too caught up in the excitement of being outside of the house to remember their cues to use the bathroom. Reminders are very helpful. Bring it up to your child, even if they do not display any signs of needing to go. It is a good rule of thumb to always take your child to the bathroom after you have any meals because this is usually when they are going to feel relaxed enough to go. Remember that children are going to have to use the bathroom more frequently than adults. You will want to remind them to use the bathroom about twice as much as you would if you were reminding an adult.

The process is going to have some ups and downs, just like any other aspect of potty training. Any guidelines that you have been following at home will also apply when you are not at home--be as patient as you can. The environment might prove to be too stressful for your child, and this might result in an accident. Get them clean and dry in order to keep moving forward. Any setbacks that are focused on have the ability to stay with your child for a long time. If this keeps happening, you will know that your child might need to use pull-ups for a little while longer.

Chapter 7
Important Skills

"Don't worry that children never listen to you; they are always watching you."

-Robert Fulghum, author

As a parent, you are responsible for teaching your child the essential skills that they will need in order to become great at potty training. While it is an individual learning experience, there are things that you can do to ensure that they are going to be prepared as possible. From learning how to clean up properly to recognizing the important cues that tell them when to go to the bathroom, you are setting them up to be more self-sufficient. Children often only need to be shown something a few times before they pick up on it. As long as you can make it interesting, your child is going to grasp these concepts surprisingly quickly. Before you know it, they will be using the bathroom on their own thanks to the skills that you have helped them acquire.

Enjoy these moments with your child because each step that you take is bringing them closer to independence. The bond that you form while you are potty training is one that cannot be compared to anything else. A lot of parents agree that they would love to go back to the potty training days once they have completed them. The process is time-consuming and a test of patience, but the end result is something that is going to benefit your child for the rest of their life. Not only will these skills allow them to feel independent, but they will also benefit their health and safety.

Learning How to Wipe

Wiping is something that takes a lot of time to master. Since children are going to be responsible for it for the first time during the potty training process, you are going to have to spend a decent amount of time going over how to do it properly to ensure that they are prepared. Wiping after peeing is something that is probably going to be a simple task to learn, but cleaning up after pooping usually proves to be more difficult for children. You will have to make sure that they are using enough toilet paper, but not too much to clog the toilet. The direction in which they wipe is also very important for health reasons. A lot of parents find it hard to guide their children during this stage, but the process doesn't have to be complex.

Use simple language, just as you have with every other aspect of potty training so far. Explain why you wouldn't want to wipe a dirty bottom from back to front, regardless of the gender of your child. Don't be shy to explain why this is a bad thing because it is much better to have this talk with your child than go through any bacterial infections that they might obtain from wiping incorrectly. You might have to remind them about wiping front to back fairly often, but this is a lot easier than having to explain the entire process of what happens when you wipe the other direction. Honesty and simplicity are important during this stage. Your child is going to be able to grasp the concept better when you explain it honestly than if you were to make up silly nicknames for what is going on.

Remember, talking to your child as though they are an adult is an automatic way to grab their attention. They are going to recognize your tone and the meaning behind the conversation. When you do this, you are placing a sense of importance in the fact that you are having this discussion. When your child picks up on these conversational cues, they are going to be keen on listening to what you have to say. This wisdom is what is going to help them succeed, so make sure that you teach them each step very carefully. Answer any questions that they have, and do not make them feel embarrassed for asking. This open level of communication is what you should always be striving for, especially while you are teaching them how to wipe properly.

Knowing exactly the right amount of toilet paper to use is a skill that is learned over time. While you can explain this to your child, it is likely that they are going to forget sometimes. This is okay because there are other alternatives that you can look into during the potty training stage. Toilet wipes are an excellent alternative to toilet paper. Much like baby wipes, they are single-use and pre-measured so that your child will not have to guess how many they should be using. The moisture also helps to get them fully cleaned. Consider keeping a pack of these toilet-safe wipes nearby as your child is being potty trained. You can even bring them with you on the go for an easier public restroom experience.

You might be at a loss for how to explain the hand placement and motion that should be used when wiping. It is not necessary to wait until your child has used the bathroom to demonstrate this. Taking toilet paper or a flushable wipe, you can show them the proper technique by simply imagining that you are going through the process. Explain to your child to wipe with the paper flat instead of crumpling it up into a ball. From there, you can then explain that they can fold the flattened dirty paper and use it again on the clean side for maximum efficiency. These tips are going to prevent wasted toilet paper and allow your child to truly get as clean as they need to. Have them practice with you, mirroring the motions that you are teaching them.

For the first few times that your child wipes on their own, it is best to walk into the bathroom and perform a quick check. It will save you the time of cleaning soiled underwear if you can walk in there to look before your child finishes up. At this point, you can provide any advice or tips on the areas that your child might be struggling in. Practice definitely makes perfect when it comes to wiping, so let them do it often. While it is faster and easier for you to do it for them, they are never going to learn unless they realize that they are the ones who are responsible for cleaning up after themselves.

Knowing When to Go

While this has already been covered in some detail within this guide, it is never a bad idea to go over the cues with your child multiple times. While you might see the signs for yourself, your child might not be aware of them. If you notice that your child is getting all of the concepts regarding potty training, yet they are still experiencing accidents, then it is likely that they need to be reminded of the cues. Explaining that the feeling of pressure inside of the stomach usually indicates that it is time to go to the bathroom is a good way to begin. Even if this feeling is simply related to gas or bloating, your child should still be sitting on the toilet and trying to go to the bathroom. You can explain that the feeling of needing to pee and needing to poop is somewhat similar, and it is not good to hold on to this feeling for too long.

In order to become more familiarized with the pressure that is felt, you can let your child press on their own stomach to see what it feels like. Warn them to press gently because the pressure can build up quickly and unexpectedly, especially if your child does need to use the bathroom already. This exploration really helps your child become knowledgeable about what the feeling is that they should be anticipating. Have them wiggle around a little bit without touching their stomach. This is another way to create the same bodily response. This dance is known as the "pee pee dance" and is a way that many children are able to gauge if they need to use the bathroom or not.

Another great reminder to provide to your child is to try to use the bathroom after eating. Waiting until the food is digesting might mean that it is too late. Explain that when you fill up your stomach with food and drinks, this pushes down any pee or poop that might need to come out. This simple visual representation is going to allow your child to remember that what goes in must eventually come out. Tell them that, even if they do not necessarily feel that they have to go after they eat, it is still a good idea to sit down on the toilet and see if anything happens.

Farting is something that should be normalized. While you do want your child to know that it is impolite to pass gas in public as long as they are in control of it, they should also know that it does happen sometimes. Farting can also be a great cue for needing to use the bathroom. If you notice that your child passes gas frequently, ask them at that moment if they feel that they need to poop. When you normalize this, it becomes less embarrassing or shameful to discuss their gas. Your child will become comfortable discussing these things with you, therefore reducing the risk of having accidents. A mistake that a lot of parents make is the idea that they must teach their children that it is never okay to fart. Not only is that unrealistic, but it can also cause the child to ignore important cues.

Be open with your child about your own needs. Since you are going to be leading by example, express when you feel that you have to use the bathroom. Without having to go into great detail, these statements can help remind your child that they might need to go as well. It will also further the open lines of communication that you strive for. This might be a struggle for you as the parent to be so candid about your own bathroom usage, but it will really help your child as they grow up. By explaining to your child that you have to go, they are going to see it as a decision that you are making. Something normally clicks in the child's brain that allows them to realize that they also have control over their own bladder and bowel movements. It is likely that they will begin to model their own behavior after yours.

An important factor to remember is that your child should know enough about their own body by the time they start displaying signs that they are ready to be potty trained. Believe in this because it can impact their confidence level if you second guess it. If you see that your child isn't mature enough to recognize any of the cues, then it is likely that potty training has probably been started too early. As you know, this does not impact your child's ability to learn how to become self-sufficient in the future. All you can do is provide encouragement until you see signs that show your child might need more time. If you have anyone else in the household or any other caregivers involved in the potty training process, remember to ask them to provide the same encouragement. Children need all of the support that they can get while they are navigating through this process.

Becoming Self-Sufficient

There comes a time as a parent when you will notice that your little one isn't so little anymore. Potty training normally brings up this feeling, and it can be a lot to handle for both the parent and the child. Being potty trained means that your child is one step closer to reaching a self-sufficient stage in life. While you always want to do all that you can for them, you have likely realized by now that it is necessary to take several steps back while they learn how to use the bathroom on their own. There is normally a bittersweet feeling that comes along with this process. Remember all of the joy that comes with the potty training process. It is one that is full of excitement and new discoveries for your child. While you might feel that they no longer need you, they are truly looking for guidance more than ever without you even realizing it.

Setting a great example is how you raise a confident and independent child who is ready to tackle any process. A lot of parents feel timid at the idea of beginning potty training because they believe that it is going to be a hard experience. While it can be hard at times, always remember that the end result is going to bring your child a lot of happiness and self-awareness. It is a necessary step in life, and it does not matter if you delay it because it is bound to happen eventually. As long as your child is ready to be potty trained by exhibiting the signs that we have gone over, then you can rest assured that your child is ready to become more self-sufficient.

There are little things that you can do for your child to help the process run more smoothly. Allowing them to get dressed and undressed on their own is one of the changes that usually take place during potty training. It is important that your child masters how to take their pants off and put them back on because it is going to be happening a lot. The more that you let them practice doing this, the better they are going to get at it. Always make the experience sound like a fun privilege in order to build up interest. Much like picking out underwear can promote a child's desire to use the bathroom on their own, so can the idea of being able to pick out an entire outfit and put it on by themselves. For the sake of ease, make sure that their clothing does not contain too many zippers or buttons. During the first few months of potty training, this is only going to cause hurdles that your child will have to overcome.

If you are using a potty chair or a children's toilet, even a stool for them to rest their feet while sitting on the toilet, make sure that your child knows where each of these items is stored. Since they are going to be the one to use them, they should have access to them at all times. While it is natural that they won't be able to set everything up on their own right away, allowing them to know how to do it and where to do it is a behavior that encourages self-sufficiency. Make sure that you encourage them to help you as you set up the bathroom for them before they use it. Becoming familiarized with this process is another way to get them invested in wanting to use the toilet. It almost seems like something that is fun to a child, plus it is another way of bonding. They will feel so proud of the moment that they are able to show you they can set everything up on their own.

After you have gone over how to wipe correctly, it might take your child some time before they feel that they can truly do it on their own. A transitional stage might be required here, and that is okay. Try to ease them into the process by encouraging them to wipe after they pee, but still helping them wipe after they poop. Again, a little encouragement goes a long way with this process. Mastering how to wipe is one of the biggest aspects of potty training other than recognizing the urge to go. It is not an easy task, but your child is going to pick up on it with a little coaxing from you.

As your child gets the hang of using the bathroom entirely independently, the reward system (if you are using one) can be tapered off. Pretty soon, you will have a toddler who knows when, how, and where to go without consulting you about it. This does not mean that the encouragement ever has to stop; make sure that you express how proud you are often. This momentum is going to keep building up and it will continually build your child up. Self-sufficiency goes beyond being able to go through the motions and extends into your child's view of themselves. If they are confident and happy, then you know that the methods you have taught them are working.

Conclusion

What you have likely realized is that there are no standard guidelines to potty training your child. It is an individualized experience that should come with a flexible attitude and many backup plans. The exciting part about potty training is that you genuinely never know what to expect, and your child just might surprise you with their ability to pick up on the methods that you teach them. There is never going to be a "perfect time" to begin potty training your child, so it is best to pay attention to the signs that they are ready and to go from there. While you can prepare ahead of time, truly all that you need to begin is a patient attitude and a clear explanation of the process.

Accidents are going to happen, but that does not need to stop either one of you from continuing with the potty training. Clean up after them and move forward. Do your best to teach your child that accidents happen so that they do not become fearful of having more in the future. As long as you are able to keep your calm demeanor, your child will know that you are not disappointed in them. By utilizing games and rewards in your teaching methods, you will be able to keep the environment fun and the mood happy. There is a lot that you can do to make the process seem less formal, yet still every bit as educational.

Talk to your child as you would to any other mature person, making sure that they know you have trust in them. If you can have this openness with your child, they are going to feel that they can come to you with any questions or concerns that they might have about potty training. No matter what happens during the process, there is always a solution to try. You might have to incorporate transitional stages into your potty training methods, but if it is working for your child, then you should know to keep doing it. By taking any fear or intimidation out of the process, both you and your child are going to have a great potty training experience.

Check out our Other *AMAZING* Titles:

1. Mindfulness Activities for Kids; Fun Ways to Keep Your Children Distracted and Reduce Stress for Your Kids and You!

You can't predict everything that your child goes through, but you can start to prepare them for life's most challenging moments. The best way to do this is to participate in mindfulness with them.

To start off, we are going to give you some ideas of things that you can do together as a family to help transition them into mindfulness. When you can work with your child to overcome their stress rather than just expecting them to do it on their own, this will be most effective.

We understand that not everyone has the time to give their child attention throughout the entire day, and it is not healthy for them anyway! However, these activities will not only keep them mindful but enable them to understand their emotions as well.

The more you and your child can participate in these activities, the healthier they will be in the end. Give your child every tool that you have to make sure that they are able to be happy and free from stress and chronic anxiety.

Nature and Identifying Walk

One of the most important things a child needs is an active lifestyle. Though they have higher metabolisms and naturally more energy than adults, they still need exercise just as much as we do. When they're deprived of the kind of healthy physical movement needed for children, then it will show negatively in their overall development.

One simple way to start to practice mindfulness is by taking a nature walk. A regular walk is great for children, but what's important about a nature walk is that you are giving them actual things that they can identify and learn from as you go on your journey together.

If your child can walk, make sure to leave the stroller in the car. It might be hard to get them to walk the entire way, but it is still good for their development to have the freedom to roam. As long as the path that you are choosing is safe, then you do not have anything to worry about with letting them explore on their own. It is especially important that you let your younger children roam. You will be watching them the entire time and giving them the chance to do some discovering while they still know that you are there to give them that sense of security needed.

Choose a place that will have a plethora of trees, plants, and rocks. It doesn't necessarily have to be a nature preserve, but it should just be something different than a normal route that they are used to walking and driving. When they are used to the same setting, they will not look for new stimuli. There are always nature walk locations wherever you are, so be sure to bring your children to these types of areas. A simple walk through your own backyard might be enough as well if there are trees, plants, and other forms of nature for them to discover.

During this walk, let them lead the way. Do they want to go left or right? Up the hill or down the lesser-used path? Do they want to go fast or slow? When you give them the ability to lead the way, you are giving them the encouragement and confidence needed to boost their self-esteem and alleviate their anxiety. You have also enabled yourself to force them into a mindful state. They have to look at the things around them and decide which way they are going to go. If you do all the leading and tell them to only follow you, they are not going to be as likely to stay present in the moment.

As you are walking around, point out different things to them. Do not tell them where to look. Simply ask them things like, "Did you see that butterfly?" or "Can you see how big and tall that tree is?" Some children are naturally defiant, so if you tell them, "Look at that over there!" they might ignore you. If they do not seem to be mindful at the moment of your walk, then you can give them prompts and ideas of things to look for. Maybe you ask them how many bugs they can see, how many birds they hear, or how many flowers they can pick. Remember to guide them through this nature walk rather than telling them exactly where they need to go.

Breathing Together

One important thing that children need to remember is how to breathe. We all breathe on our own without even having to think about it. Even when you are sleeping your lungs continue to work hard to bring the air into your body, cycle it, and send it right back out. Your children's body does this as well. However, if we let our emotions take over, this means that they might take over our lungs as well! It can be easy to get lost in heavy breathing when you are upset. Think about the last time that you cried. It was very challenging to manage your breathing! Your child will have this same struggle as well when they are upset.

Often, the reason that kids cry so hard and continue to be upset is simply because they are already crying. The idea of being sad and scared takes over their brain, and they will continue to be upset until they are able to remove themselves from the situation or get the exact thing that they might be crying about. We can't always provide our children with the specific things that they need, so it is essential that we ensure we teach our children how to naturally calm down in any given scenario. This will involve healthy breathing activities.

To start, make sure that you are counting down with them. When you count up, it can give them a sense that something is building, like something might happen at 10. When you count down from ten, you give them a better sense that something is ending. It will give them the feeling that it is okay to slow down and stop the feelings that they're having so that you can both have a healthy discussion of what's really going on.

A good method is to hold their hands as you both count down from them. Have them breathe in for five, and out for five. So, as you count, they would breathe in for ten, nine, eight, seven, six, and then out for five, four, three, two, and one. Have them repeat this until they've stopped crying or feeling incredibly anxious.

Another good method is to have them start to breathe in through their nose and out through their mouths. By focusing your breathing like this, you are already being mindful. Make sure that you do the breathing exercise with them. If you just tell them that they need to breathe, then they are going to reject that because it can feel overwhelming to be told what to do when they are already having an emotional breakdown. Breathe with them so they can see that it works, they know how to do it, and they feel comfort and support from you.

When these basic exercises are not working, you can try something a little more complex. A good yoga method of breathing is to use your thumb and pinkie to alternate which nostril you breathe through. This is a perfect method to use when your child is feeling anxious or nervous. It starts by making a fist with your right hand, and sticking your thumb and pinky out. Take your right pinky and place it over your left nostril. Breathe in as you count down from five through your right nostril. Then, place your right thumb over this right nostril, releasing your right pinky and breathing out as you count down from five. It is an easy mindfulness activity that you can do anywhere and anytime with your child to help them really calm down and cool off from the things that are taking all their attention and causing stress.

Gratitude Discussion

Anxiety causes us to see the things that we do not have rather than the things that we do. Gratitude is a practice of being thankful and appreciative of what you already have now. It is not just positive thinking, it is the recognition of the greatness in one's life. Even if everything is seemingly terrible, there are always things that we have to be grateful for. When you have moments to talk and discuss with your child, it is important to remember to discuss gratitude.

This is sometimes done with religious children who might say thanks and pray before bedtime, but it is not something strictly associated with a religion. You should have them discuss what they are happy for, what excited them, and what's most important in their life at any given moment. When they have this opportunity, they will be able to be happier even in times of great stress. The best time to have these conversations is when they might be bored in the car, when you are eating dinner, when you are hanging out on the couch, or before bed as you are tucking them in. It is a great habit to include in your child's life from the start when you can ask them what they are thankful for and how this has positively impacted their life.

One great way to do this is when you are enjoying a family meal together. You can go around the table and each share one thing that they are thankful for that they experienced that day. We often wait until certain holidays like Thanksgiving to really share these kinds of positive ideas about our life with others. Do not feel like this is the only time that you can show thanks! You should try to do this as often as possible. Sometimes we need to practice gratitude as adults. If you do not know what you have gratitude for and how to recognize that in your life, it will be harder for your child to understand as well.

The first thing that you can discuss with gratitude is through health. Discuss how they should have gratitude over being able to walk up and down the stairs, go for a run and play, move their arms to dance, and

69

do other things that involve using your entire body. Remind them of the gratitude they should have for being able to see amazing things, hear their favorite songs, and talk to share their thoughts and opinions. Remind them of how thankful they should be for tasty food, things that smell good, and the fun times they can have when going out to eat and things like that. Remind them of the thanks they should have for their toys and all the other personal belongings they have. Remind them of the family and friends who love them so dearly, and how happy and grateful they are to have this in their life. These are all things that we can practice gratitude over as adults as well.

Do not try to prove to your children that they need to be grateful based on what other people might be lacking. Do not tell them, "You should be grateful for your legs because there are other kids in wheelchairs." Don't say, "You need to have gratitude for your food because there are kids starving in the world." You might end up making them feel guilty, and this could potentially cause stress. Do not base around what they should be happy for over what others are lacking. Instead, make them grateful on their own as an individual. You might say something like, "Are you not happy to have two legs to take you anywhere you want? Is it not fun that we get to eat all these snacks and tasty foods?" Ask them questions to get them thinking of the things that they're grateful for on their own.

Alternatively, make sure that you are not forcing these ideas onto them. Sometimes they can be more stressed or have higher feelings of guilt when they feel pressured into thinking a certain way. The best way to teach them gratitude is by showing it. Let it be a part of your language. Point out when you are feeling overwhelmed with joy and gratitude because they will pick up on it. Reflect as often as you can and make sure that they are coming up with their own ideas of what they are thankful for as well.

Mindful Meals

Eating together with your entire family can be really difficult sometimes. Trying to get everyone in the same room and eating all the things that we each like to eat can seem like a puzzle game that's impossible to figure out. However, eating together is one of the most important things that you can do for you and your child's health. In certain cultures, entire days are spent around preparing a meal and enjoying it as a family. When we have a 40-hour a week job, multiple after school activities, homework and other hobbies that we do at night, it seems like there is no time to eat. This is when it becomes easier to boil some pasta and other packaged dinners to help fill them up for the day. This is fine to do in moderation, but we still need to put an emphasis on mindful meals. It can also seem impossible to keep them at the dinner table, but it is one of the most important things that you could ever do for them. Having regular meals together can be just as important for their health as other things that they participate in.

One of the healthiest diets in the world is the Mediterranean diets. You've likely heard of this at some point, maybe as a way to lose weight. Beyond that, a Mediterranean diet is one that helps to fight off certain diseases, prevent illnesses, and elongate one's life. This diet is inclusive of lots of green veggies, antioxidant fruits, whole grains, and little processed foods. It is a diet based around people who live around the Mediterranean sea. It was discovered that these populations lived the longest and had fewer health conditions when compared geographically to other locations. When looking at their diet, it is clear to see that these healthy foods are very important to include in one's diet. However, what is it about this diet that is different than other regular meal plans that call for lots of fruits and veggies and fewer processed foods? Why not just go on a vegetarian diet or something else that emphasizes the same kinds of foods?

The thing that really sets those who live in the Mediterranean apart is that many people in these kinds of cultures will put an emphasis on eating together. Meals are not just a half hour quick thing. They are activities that include the whole family and require everyone to sit down and reflect as they are eating. It is not always about what food you are eating that will affect your health, but how you are eating. You have an extra hour a day to spare for your family. You have the time to sit down together. It is not just about actually bringing the entire family to sit down just to eat either.

Everyone can play a role in the preparation. Sometimes it is overwhelming to cook a meal for the whole family because that's a lot of food for one person to have to cook! However, everyone can play a role in preparing a meal. Have older kids help to chop veggies. The little kids can set the table and gather the right dishes. A spouse can take over some cooking duties. Though you might be the only one who can cook in the family and everyone else burns toast without even trying, you can still delegate tasks. It is a team building way to make sure that everyone is contributing. After dinner is over, everyone can help clean up. When everyone is involved, it makes the process go so much smoother. Let the kids decide what they want to do. Sometimes it is hard to get them to participate because they do not feel like it. They might simply reject your attempts at trying to get them to help. Rather than telling them exactly what they need to do, give them a chance to pick out their own tasks. Ask if they want to help chop veggies, boil pasta, set the table, and so on. Each of these tasks only takes a few minutes, but when you are doing it all on your own, it can take hours! You have all these hands in your family that can help, so put in the effort to make sure that they are participating.

When it comes to the actual dinner, make sure that you are being mindful during this time. You do not have to do a strict "no phones" rule because this can make some teens check-out and not care about the meal. Just have them limit their phone use. Turn off the TV and listen to some classical or other calming music. Keep everyone engaged by having discussions.

There are a few things you shouldn't discuss and a few things that you should emphasize when having a happy dinner. Never discuss stressful things between you and your spouse. Though it might be the only time that you two can talk about a loan you have to take out, finding a new job, or issues with insurance, try to wait this out. Do not hide these things as we discussed earlier, but there is a time and place to have more serious adult conversations. Do not use this time for discipline or punishment either, especially if you have multiple children. You do not want to point one out and make them feel bad about themselves in front of everyone. If they got a bad grade, got in trouble at school, and so on, wait until you can have a one on one discussion with them.

Do discuss their days. Ask everyone how things went, what fun things happened, and some issues they might have run into. You do not only have to talk positively at the table! It can be helpful to get through issues as a family. However, you do need to be mindful about heated arguments. Just ensure that when challenging things are being discussed, everyone is mindful and listening healthily, not trying to get into a fight or punish each other.

One activity that you can do at the dinner table is ask one thing that you are grateful for, as mentioned in the previous section. In addition to this, consider asking them one new thing they learned that day. It forces your children to go back to their day and reflect on the new information that they were given. Maybe it is something interesting from class, something they learned from a friend, or an important lesson that they experienced. It is a perfect way to keep everyone mindful in the moment.

Another activity is to ask them what the high and low was in the day. What was the best thing that they experienced? What might have they gone through that wasn't the greatest? What challenges did they face or what accomplishments did they make? Do not wait for Thanksgiving to discuss important things in their life!

Even if you bring McDonald's home for dinner, that's okay! Still emphasize sitting down at the table so you can talk and discuss together. You might not be able to do this every day, but several times a week it should be your priority to eat together. Start to treat every meal like a holiday meal and you will discover that your family's anxiety can be reduced.

Making a Mood Chart

It can be incredibly challenging for children to know how to properly express their emotions. Sometimes they do not have the right vocabulary to share their feelings, and there are certain situations where they might not even know what it is that they are feeling. It is very helpful to think of a nonverbal way to start to express feelings, especially with younger children. This is an activity meant for kids under 10 or so, as preteens and older will have better ways of verbalizing their feelings. When you can give children the means to understand what it is that they are emotionally feeling, they will be able to work through that in a happy and healthy way. Even as adults, we are limited to describing our feelings and emotional experiences through words that we know. To really understand what you are dealing with, we need more ways of communicating the things that we are feeling. Sometimes you do not even realize your feelings until after they've already happened!

To start this mindfulness activity out with children, decide what your medium for your chart is going to be. You can use a big poster board to keep in their room, or maybe instead you use a journal to record your feelings. Little kids will probably do better with a big visual that they can play with. From there, you will want to create a chart like a calendar. You might need to make a new one every month, but you can also use something like a dry erase board or a chalkboard so that you can change it as needed.

What is most important in this aspect is having a "mood key." It will be like a key on a map with different things that will help them to express the emotions that they are feeling. You will want to list the emotions that they will feel and then a symbol to go along with that word. This way, they are associating a feeling with something symbolic that will be easier to communicate for little ones who do not always remember all their words.

You will want to list out basic emotions such as fear, sadness, anger, frustration, jealousy, impatience, and so on. You will then want to list positive emotions as well because it is just as crucial that they are aware of all the things that make them feel good. These are things like excitement, happiness, fun, and so on. You can list all of these out and talk with them about what each means. Use real situations that you have gone through to help them understand what the word means. Then, you will want to come up with your symbol. This could be something as easy as a smiley face or a frowny face. You can use simple shapes that are different shades of colors as well. This is for you and your child to determine.

Once you have done this, keep that key with you, or something like it, when you can. When your child is having a mood and you are not sure what it is, you can pull out the mood chart. You can show them the symbols and have them pick out which one they are feeling to help them through a challenging time. They will then start to associate their moods with the symbols, getting a better understanding of how they are feeling. You can help them through this emotion, and they will be able to associate that positive resolution with that emotion they might be feeling.

The calendar can also be something that you keep to yourself if you want to track your child's moods, but it is good for them to see it as well. At the end of the day, or a couple times that day, you can mark the calendar with the different moods they might have felt. Even if they were happy and excited all day, you can have them mark this down. The point of the calendar is to help show your children what moods they experienced in the past so they can associate that with an experience. It will be easier for them to discover their different triggers on their own this way and give them a visualization of the things that they feel so that they can be happier and healthier later on.

Creating an Anxiety Token

When your child is feeling anxious without you, it can be even scarier. This is especially true if they are going to be around a relative or other caretaker who is not as sensitive to their different needs as you might be. To give them something that they can keep with them all the time to help reduce their anxiety, you should come up with an anxiety token. What this involves is having something that they can touch and hold when they are feeling anxious. It is a reminder that everything is going to be okay, and that they will be able to get through their scarier emotions on their own. This is something that adults can find to be useful as well!

For this activity, make sure that you are doing it together and not just giving them the supplies to do it on their own. You will want to purchase a few different colors of molding clay, the kind that you can either let air dry to harden or bake. Just ensure that it is not clay that will dry out. Discuss why you are doing this with your child. Let them know that you want to provide them with something that will alleviate their anxiety when they need to the most. Remind them that their emotions are okay, but sometimes they will have to get through them on their own. Let them know that you will always be there to support them, and when you are not around, they will still have the capabilities to work through these things independently.

Next, decide what colors your child would like to use. You will be making a simple clay ball, about the size of a grape. You can use a few different colors that you can swirl together, you can use one simple color that you add things like glitter to, or you can come up with your own pattern! You can make more than one anxiety token as well to let your child know that if they ended up losing it, it wouldn't be the end of the world. You can keep these in a jar by the front door so they can always remember to grab one on the way to work.

Now it is time for you to make the ball with your child. This is the perfect time to talk about their anxiety and what makes them scared. You can talk about stress, frustration, anger, and impatience. You can remind them that this is something that they will use to remember the good times. They can hold this token in their hand and remind themselves that everything is going to work out, they will be okay, and they are strong enough to power through their emotions. By doing this, you remind them to reflect on the past. You encourage them to look at the things that they've been through to remember what it is like to work through these kinds of feelings.

After you have crafted the perfect colorful fun ball, press it flat so it is about the thickness of an Oreo cookie. It should be around this size, or smaller, nice and smooth and flat. Then, have your child press their thumb into the clay just once. Bake it or let it set and there you have it! Whenever they are stressed or scared, they can press their thumb into this token and have something that will make them mindful.

Encourage them to share it with others as well! Let them know that if they see one of their friends anxious or scared, they can share this if they want. They can give it to a friend and talk to them about their emotions. If you enable your child to be self-aware enough to be able to help other children work through their feelings, you are going to be at a Rockstar level of parenting!

Remind them that they can use this token when they are really happy as well. We shouldn't only reflect on negative emotions. It is important to remind ourselves that we are feeling happy when we have good moments so that we can remember these times to get us through the tough stuff. The token is going to be a way to pull them from their thoughts and bring them right back to reality.

If you really want to get creative, you can use several different color-coordinated tokens to help out. You might have a red one, a purple one, and a blue one. They can carry the red one with them when they are having a creative day and want to do something fun and wild! The blue one might be when they are feeling angry and having a day where every little thing irritates them. The purple one can be for times of peace when they want to just relax and have a chill day. These tokens can signify their feelings and let other family members know what might be going on in their minds. It can be their way of expressing their emotions in a nonverbal way. Remind them that they do not need to stick to just one colored token for the day either! If they start their day with the blue and only use that throughout the day, it might make them feel as though they need to stay in that bad mood even if they start to get pulled from it. Remind them that their emotions are not permanent, and that they can always ground themselves back in the present with the anxiety token.

Want to read more? Check out our full book on **Mindfulness Activities for Kids** *on Amazon today!*

2. Anger Management in Children; Helping Your Child Express Anger In A Positive Way

The Triggers

Before you can start addressing your child's anger issues, you must first identify his triggers. What are the reasons behind why he's acting out in the first place? A lot of parents are often bewildered when their child starts acting out and are disappointed with his behavior. They might feel like they are walking on an emotional minefield where anything seems to set their child off. This is not an easy thing to deal with, and a lot of parents feel hopeless and even defeated. However, the good news is that you can turn things around, not just for yourself but for your child as well.

A circumstance or feeling is never the cause of the problem, and it is your child's reaction to them that causes the problems. It is essential to identify the problem if you want to come up with an effective solution to cope with this issue. What sets your child off? This is one question you must carefully answer. Once you identify the triggers, handling the matter becomes rather easy. A trigger can be almost anything including an event or situation that leads to an anger tantrum. The only way to help your child control and regulate his behavior is by coming up with a list of triggers.

In terms of behavior management, a trigger is referred to as a situation that leads to an inappropriate response or reaction to that situation. Simply put, the feeling or the situation is never the problem. Instead, it is the way the child views and feels about these things and his internal self-talk that causes trouble. If the child doesn't have the skills to efficiently and effectively respond to or manage a trigger, he will start acting out. For instance, he might become angry and think to himself, "This is not fair; I don't have to deal with this." This kind of thinking is common among tweens or teenagers and is referred to as negative self-talk. Negative self-talk invariably leads to an angry outburst or tantrum.

At times, your child might not act out immediately and might instead resort to passive behavior. Think of such instances or situations where you might have been talking to your child for over 10 minutes, and he pretends like he hasn't been listening to you. Children often do this, and it is known as passive-aggressive behavior. In such situations, your child's internal self-talk is something along these lines: "I don't have to listen to what others tell me. I can do what I want, and no one can control me."

This self-talk is the reason why your child is visibly ignoring you. Some children tend to act out, whereas others tend to act in. They withdraw into their own shell, shut others out, or refuse to talk to anyone who is trying to understand what went wrong with them. They're essentially engaging in negative self-talk that makes them feel helpless.

The first step toward helping your child get a better understanding of his emotions and regulate them is to learn about his triggers. Once you learn about his triggers, it becomes easier to talk to him about them. When you can identify and recognize his triggers, he can effectively learn to manage them, as well. All the anger management techniques discussed in this book will not work if you don't identify his triggers. This process is not easy, and it requires a lot of discussions about problem-solving. It takes time, consistent effort, and repetition before he can finally get the hang of it. So, please be patient with him and encourage him to do the same too.

There are two simple steps you must follow to identify your child's triggers, and they are as follows.

Observation and investigation

The best tool at your disposal to understand your child's anger triggers is observation. This is especially helpful when dealing with younger children who don't have a lot of self-awareness. You must be attentive and watch out for any warning signs. Carefully watch and listen when your child is spending time with his friends at home, playing outside, or doing his homework. After a while, you will start to see a couple of patterns. For instance, your child might enjoy his daily reading but might not like doing his math homework. As soon as it is time for him to get down to business and do his math homework, he might start getting restless, visibly agitated, and he may even throw a tantrum. So, in such a situation, one trigger you have successfully identified is his homework. Or, you might notice that your child starts acting a little moody once he gets home from the playground. This might be a trigger related to an issue he's having with his friends. Be alert and start looking for patterns. Remember, at this stage, you are merely observing, and you're not trying to investigate the issue. If you start going through his stuff or spying on him, you will not help the situation. Instead, try to be upfront and talk to him about your observations.

If you want, you can also ask other adults your child interacts with to observe his general behavior. You can enlist the help of your relatives, his teachers, or even other parents who interact with him. If your child has angry outbursts around other adults, ask them if they saw anything or heard anything before the reaction. If your child got into trouble because of his anger issues at school, talk to his teachers and try to identify the reason behind his behavior. Once you realize there are some patterns, you can start investigating. Start talking to others who are involved in your child's life and get their input. Once you piece together all the information you have obtained, it becomes easier to understand your child's behavior and his triggers. You will need all the help you can get.

Perception matters

You must factor in perception along with your observations. The way your child perceives a situation guides his reaction to it. The way he handles and understands things is quite different from the way you do. You might think you know what happened or what went wrong, but your child might experience the same situation quite differently. So, don't assume that you have all the answers. Instead, factor in his responses and perception before coming to any conclusions.

Let us assume that your child got into trouble at school because he pushed another kid down on the playground. Before you start reprimanding him, ask him, "Why did you push the other kid?" Some children might not be able to fully articulate their reasons for their behavior, but it is worth trying. Before you continue with this question and answer session, give him some time to calm down. Once he is calm and relaxed, you can start a discussion about it. When doing this, remember you are trying to understand what's going on in his mind. Don't jump to any conclusions and don't be judgmental; instead, allow him to talk. Be a good listener and don't keep interrupting him. Emotions aren't always easy to express especially for children, so give your child an opportunity to express himself.

Explain About Triggers

Now that you are aware of the various factors that trigger your child's temper, it is time to help him understand them himself. Before he can identify his triggers, he must understand what the word itself means. You can easily explain what a trigger means to an adult, but explaining it to a child might be tricky. Anything that elicits a reaction from your child is a trigger. For instance, when you tickle your child, he will laugh. So, tickling is the trigger, and laughter is the reaction. To make things clear, go ahead and tickle your child. As he starts to laugh, he will understand the meaning of a trigger. After this, you can go ahead and explain what anger triggers mean.

Any action, situation, emotion, or anything else that makes your child angry is his trigger. The most common triggers for anger in children include anxiety, a sense of injustice, tiredness, frustration, or lack of sleep. However, this list isn't exhaustive, and there can be various triggers.

Awareness About Triggers

In this section, you will learn about a couple of simple tips you can use to help your child understand and become aware of his triggers.

Identify the triggers

There is a direct relation between feelings and triggers. So, talking about feelings can help identify your child's triggers. This is especially helpful if you're dealing with a young child. Don't attempt to do this while your child is in the middle of an angry outburst or while he is throwing a tantrum. When your child is calm, ask him why he was angry, and what made him angry? Ask him about the things that make him happy and sad. Mainly, you're teaching him the difference between various emotions and helping him identify what he was feeling. It also is a great way to show him that regardless of what he is feeling, there is no excuse for him to act poorly. Explaining triggers also encourages him to start effectively communicating his feelings to you.

Connecting the dots

Tell your child about your various observations and the reasons you think he behaved the way he did. Here is a simple way to go about it: "I have noticed that whenever you think something is ___, you tend to get visibly upset." By helping him connect the dots, you are making it easier for him to identify his triggers. In this type of problem-solving, you must actively engage in discussion with your child, and you must not exclude him from this discussion. There will be different ways in which you think your child can handle his triggers. Well, even your child might have a couple of ideas. You can both compare your notes and come up with an effective strategy to help manage his triggers in the future. This will also allow you to connect with your child, and he will feel like his ideas or opinions are valid too.

The signs

Usually, a trigger comes along with a couple of physical symptoms. For instance, if you are angry about something, your heartbeat rises, blood rushes to your face, and your muscles can get tense. Whenever a trigger is present in the immediate surroundings, your child's nervous system tends to kick into high gear, and he might experience the symptoms mentioned above. Talk to him about the signs and ask your child if he has ever experienced any of these feelings when the trigger you were talking about in the previous step is present. Once your child starts to become aware of the various physical cues his body is giving him, it becomes easier for him to start managing his anger.

Come up with cues

A simple behavioral management technique you can use is cueing. Select a specific trigger to work with, and come up with a cue (a hand gesture, signal, or a phrase) to help alert your child about the presence of a trigger. This helps make the child conscious of his behavior and his internal feelings. It is also a great way to help your child cope with his emotions, especially in social settings. Once your child is alert to the presence of the trigger, he has a chance to control his reaction and respond accordingly. You can use this technique while at home as well.

Checking in

If you gave your child the cue, and he didn't respond the way he was supposed to, talk to him about it later. Perhaps you can excuse yourself and talk to him about what is going on with him. Find a quiet spot and do a quick check-in to see what went wrong. This is an opportunity for you to correct your child's behavior and help him manage his anger. Remind him about your game plan once again and tell him about the consequences if he doesn't follow the game plan.

It is not an easy process to teach your child about his triggers. If you really want your child to become aware of his triggers, you will need to work on it consistently, and a lot of repetition is required. It requires commitment from you as well as your child. It doesn't make any sense if you have long heartfelt discussions and do nothing about it. You must not only come up with a plan of action but must also ensure that he sticks to it. In the meanwhile, you must be calm, loving, supportive, and keep an open dialogue about his triggers. A child must feel comfortable to talk to you about his issues, and you must not chide him when he does. A child's mind often comes up with ways to justify his behavior, and he might even get defensive in this process. Instead of reprimanding him with severe consequences, talk to him about it and explain why you must start managing his emotions.

Once your child realizes that he can manage his triggers and control his reactions, he will be more confident in himself.

Want to read more? Check out our full book on **Anger Management in Children** *on Amazon today!*

References

Famous Quotes About Children. (2019). Retrieved September 25, 2019, from https://www.compassion.com/poverty/famous-quotes-about-children.htm

How To Teach Kids To Recognize The Urge To Pee - Pull-Ups®. (2019). Retrieved September 24, 2019, from https://www.pull-ups.com/en-us/potty-training/know-when-to-go/recognize-the-urge

Markham, L. (2018, July 11). Using punishment during potty training can backfire, mama. Retrieved September 24, 2019, from https://www.mother.ly/child/using-punishment-during-potty-training-can-backfire-mama

Nair, A. (2019, January 5). 15 Best Potty Training Games to Play with Toddler. Retrieved September 24, 2019, from https://parenting.firstcry.com/articles/15-potty-training-games-for-toddlers/

Potty training: How to get the job done. (2017, November 22). Retrieved September 24, 2019, from https://www.mayoclinic.org/healthy-lifestyle/infant-and-toddler-health/in-depth/potty-training/art-20045230

Sager, J. (2014, June 23). When a Potty-Trained Kid Has Accidents: 12 Dos & Don'ts. Retrieved September 24, 2019, from https://thestir.cafemom.com/toddlers_preschoolers/173970/when_a_pottytrained_kid_has

Santomero, A., & Reber, D. (2018, April 7). 403 Forbidden. Retrieved September 24, 2019, from https://www.tipsonlifeandlove.com/parenting/shouldnt-use-baby-talk-child-heres

Teach Kids How to Wipe - Tips, Tricks and an Activity. (2018, May 31). Retrieved September 24, 2019, from https://www.kandookids.com/blog/teach-kids-how-to-wipe/

Wood, S. (2019a). 6 Potty Training Methods. Retrieved September 24, 2019, from https://www.parenting.com/toddler/potty-training/potty-training-methods/

Made in the USA
Monee, IL
26 May 2020